Finding PASSION *and* PURPOSE

FOR SERVING A LOVING GOD

We are called to a lifestyle of ministry and evangelism with expectations of serving God's purpose with passion.

Keith Edward Brownfield

New York

Finding PASSION *and* PURPOSE

by Keith Edward Brownfield

ISBN 978-1-61448-121-8 Paperback
ISBN 978-1-61448-122-5 eBook
Library of Congress Control Number: 2011940332

Published by:
Morgan James Publishing
The Entrepreneurial Publisher
5 Penn Plaza, 23rd Floor
New York City, New York 10001
(212) 655-5470 Office
(516) 908-4496 Fax
www.MorganJamesPublishing.com

Cover Design by:
Rachel Lopez
rachel@r2cdesign.com

Interior Design by:
Bonnie Bushman
bbushman@bresnan.net

In an effort to support local communities, raise awareness and funds, Morgan James Publishing donates one percent of all book sales for the life of each book to Habitat for Humanity.

Get involved today, visit
www.HelpHabitatForHumanity.org.

DEDICATIONS

This book is dedicated to all the Christians throughout America who have worked so hard in the church renewal ministry the past four decades to help thousands of laity find their own passion and purpose for serving God.

A special dedication is rendered to Bob and Phyllis Foy of Mooresville, North Carolina for their many years of sacrificial leadership while serving as National Missionaries for Church Renewal (NAMB/SBC).

A personal dedication is given to my wife Lorre for her encouragement, support, and patience during the time of this writing. I thank God daily for bringing her into my life.

TABLE OF CONTENTS

PREFACE

Some time ago, a friend of mine testified that when he joined his church, the pastor welcomed him and told him to have a seat in the pew. He did just that—sat in the pew for years, believing that following Christ simply meant faithfully attending church, listening to sermons, and singing songs of praise.

According to national statistics, most church members are doing the same thing. We are spiritually lifeless beings trying to worship God with our minds and not our hearts. I believe it's because we just don't feel any incentive to go beyond church or Sunday School attendance and discover a serious reason for accepting and following a living God. Why are we so willing to believe but not follow? Could it be because believing gets us a ticket to heaven, but following Him requires a more serious commitment that we do not want?

I see the problem as threefold. First, we respect our own privacy so much that we don't want to encroach on the privacy of others with spiritual matters. Our own lifestyle, and the secular world's pressure to be open and accepting of everyone else's lifestyle, doesn't leave us much room for reaching out to others as the apostles did.

Second, many churches offer little specific instruction or encouragement from the pulpit to find a ministry beyond attending Sunday School and the worship service. Unfortunately, many leaders seem to be more concerned about increasing or maintaining their attendance figures.

Third, even when such Bible studies and discipleship classes exist, a closer look still reveals a chasm between study and service. We laypeople have no good excuse for our unwillingness to respond to Jesus' commands to reach out to others. If we are just "lukewarm," like the church of Laodicea in the Book of Revelation, Jesus suggests a way to correct our attitude: *"Therefore, be zealous and repent"* (Rev. 3:19).

I spent many years, like my friend, sitting in a pew, neither knowing nor acknowledging that my spiritual life should be more active. But now I have a different perspective on how to live out my faith in a loving God. Thanks to His calling on my life over two decades ago, I now have a specific purpose in following the teaching of our Lord Jesus, the Christ. I have been able to move beyond believing in Jesus Christ to following Jesus Christ in ministry. That simply means that I am maturing spiritually. I have a willingness to follow Him that comes from the heart and reflects an inner drive to share His truth with others. We are all called to do that—help each other along the path to complete our spiritual journey. My drive to teach and share includes helping laity restore the passion and purpose they once had when they first accepted Jesus as their Lord and Savior.

Jesus asked Saint John to pen this letter to the church in Ephesus: *"I know your good works, your labor, and your endurance, and that you cannot tolerate evil. You have tested those who call themselves apostles and are not, and you have found them to be liars. You also possess endurance and have tolerated many things because of My name, and have not grown weary. But I have this against you: you have abandoned the love you had at first"* (Rev. 2:2-4).

After visiting more than fifty-five churches in the southeastern United States over the last few years, I'm convinced that this letter could very well be written to many of our churches today. We are doing many things right, yet we're still holding something back. What is this "first love" that Jesus accuses us of abandoning? I believe it's the passion that we first had for Him that caused us to want to accept Him into our heart, which thus enabled our purpose: to follow His footsteps as disciples. But whether it was lack of clear teaching, encouragement, or our own willingness to obey our Lord, we seem to have forgotten our purpose in life, which is to share our passion for Him with others in a meaningful way. We seem to know the will of God, but choose not to obey it.

If we Christians are going to change the world, we need to renew both the passion and purpose that we once had for Jesus Christ and begin sharing Him with others.

I invite you to join me on this spiritual journey to find your own passion and purpose in Jesus Christ.

In Acts 1:8, Jesus uttered these last words before His ascension: *"You will receive power when the Holy Spirit has come upon you."* We have the power of God in us! What is holding us back?

It's never too late to be what you should have been.
Dale Collie, author and speaker

*Following Christ calls for radical discipleship —
denying self and discarding the wisdom of the world for
the wisdom of God.*
Charles Stanley, author, pastor, theologian

Part One

THE SPIRITUAL LIFE JOURNEY

The Spiritual Life Journey is a lifelong process that takes us from the moment of salvation to an eternity with our Father in heaven. It encompasses the heart feelings leading up to our decision to accept Jesus Christ as our Savior, the development of a personal relationship with Him, and the struggle to find the passion and purpose for our life. Along the way, we'll learn to change from being a church spectator to being an active participant in the Christian life. We will learn to have a personal relationship with Jesus that will move us beyond a mere belief in Him to the full knowledge of his existence and his redemptive plan for those who believe.

Chapter 1

BEGINNING THE JOURNEY

He will transform the body of our humble condition
into the likeness of His glorious body, by the power that
enables Him to subject everything to Himself.

Philippians 3:21

In 1952, I felt a nagging feeling in my heart to improve my life. I wasn't quite a teenager yet, but I still felt that there was a better life ahead of me. I needed something in my life that I wasn't getting from my parents or my siblings. I needed Jesus!

I spoke to my youth leader, then the pastor. After several meetings with them, I accepted Jesus Christ into my life and became baptized in the faith. It indeed changed my life. I no longer struggled with disappointments, I could control my anger, and my relationships with others improved. I was excited, full of passion for Jesus, and ready to change the world! All I needed was a purpose—a direction in which to funnel that passion that I could share with others.

Throughout my teenage years, I grew in my faith, but still, that purpose I sought was missing. As I look back, I believe the proper training and mentoring that should have occurred did not. If it did occur, I missed it. Perhaps I was too inattentive to learn? Yet I still felt the passion to grow spiritually.

When I graduated from high school, I enlisted in the United States Air Force. I quickly got caught up in the activities of being on my own and began to neglect my spiritual life. Soon, habits of skipping church and running with the wrong crowds dominated my life. Yet I knew I still had the core values that were taught to me as a young man. I began to believe that those core values would sustain me and my good deeds would be rewarded. How much I had forgotten!

After many years of wandering in the wilderness, I began to feel that nagging pull on my heart once again. I knew I needed to get right with Jesus, but I just couldn't give up the relaxed lifestyle that I thought I was enjoying so much. God certainly fixed that! Over two decades ago, God called me to join a church. I soon learned that many in the congregation were just like me, struggling to find their faith. Relationships began to develop and I felt right at home with my new friends. Once again, God put me in a position to experience His work firsthand. A small group of us men began to provide work assistance to families throughout South Carolina who were both desperate and destitute. Finally I began to experience the joy of serving!

Apparently this work was not enough for a God who had a larger plan for me. I recalled the words of the prophet Jeremiah, *"For I know the plans I have for you . . . plans for your welfare, not for disaster, to give you a future and a hope.*

You will call to Me and come and pray to Me, and I will listen to you" (Jer. 29:11).

I was asked to co-teach a group of middle school students during the Sunday School hour. I struggled through those few years but I will never forget the kids who taught me so much about growing spiritually while showing mercy and forgiveness to one who was learning how to become a teacher.

This initial teaching experience led to leadership roles in discipleship training and more Sunday School teaching. God was certainly using me now! I finally had found a purpose through which to channel my passion. In the years since, I have continued to grow spiritually, but I know that I'm still a work in progress as far as God is concerned. My teaching techniques have improved and my leadership skills have developed. Still, there is always that desire to do more.

When God called me out of the wilderness to work for Him, He challenged me with different assignments. Each time, I knew that as long as He was with me and leading the way, I would succeed—as long as I didn't get in the way. Paul's encouragement to the church at Philippi, *"I am able to do all things through Him who strengthens me"* (Phil. 4:13), has proven to be so true in my life.

Along the way, I learned four things: 1) I have a spiritual gift; 2) God has specifically called me to ministry; 3) I am ably equipped for any ministry God chooses for me; and 4) I need to have a personal relationship with Jesus Christ.

The late Dr. Adrian Rogers once told the story of a businessman who told him, "I used to believe that Jesus Christ died on the cross and that He was buried and rose again, but I don't believe it anymore." Then he continued, "I don't believe it anymore. Now, I know it!" Oh, if we all could just move from the believing to the knowing! What a difference in our life, and in our relationship with Jesus Christ.

In Matthew 16, Jesus asked, *"Who do people say that the Son of Man is?"* After hearing various responses from the disciples, He asked again, *"But you, who do you say that I am?"* Peter correctly answered, *"You are the Messiah, the Son of the living God."* Peter got it right, even though his statement could have resulted in death. He had just moved from merely believing in Jesus Christ to knowing *who* He is.

If we are to find, or restore, our passion and purpose for loving Christ as He first loved us, we must all quit believing Jesus is the Messiah and start *knowing* that He is our Savior. He commands us to serve. If we truly know Him, how can we say no?

Do all the good you can, in all the ways you can, to all the souls you can, in every place you can, at all the times you can, with all the zeal you can, as long as ever you can.

John Wesley, preacher and theologian

The secret of the Christian's passion is simple: Everything we do in life we do it as to the Lord and not to men.

David Jeremiah, Christian author and pastor

Chapter 2

CHURCH SPECTATORS

For where your treasure is, there your heart will be also.

Matthew 6:21

Statistics show that the great majority of us church attendees choose to sit in the chair or pew and watch the worship time unfold. We listen to the sermon, sing the songs, and hear the prayers offered by our leaders. Beyond the worship hour, we choose to go about our lives and think no more of what we heard, witnessed, or sang at our church. Our time is our time while God's time seems to be reserved for Sunday mornings. We choose to be spectators rather than active participants.

I have many friends who pay thousands of dollars every year to attend and support the local university's football team. They have a great passion for spending their Saturdays at the stadium, tailgating and watching the game. If the team wins, they have bragging rights all week long until the next game. If the team loses, "we'll get 'em next time."

Too many of us church members choose to treat our church, and thus Jesus Christ who is the reason for church, like a football game. We come to watch! Is it enough to just give money to the church and not participate in its activities? Or are we called to be obedient to Scripture, which tells us we are called to a lifestyle of ministry and evangelism?

Now I admit it is very exciting to watch good football players make great plays. We spectators often fantasize about being that player and reacting to the jubilation of the crowd when we perform well. We are all on the team even if we are only the "twelfth man"— the fans. We choose to be spectators. That way we never get hurt. Yet we tell our friends how well we played when we win or how we could have done better if only we had chosen a different play at a critical time in the game.

I look at the football team and see sixty to eighty players suited up and ready to play. We know that the coach will only use a few of those players in every game. He chooses the best players available because his goal is to win the game. The rest of the players sit on the bench and wait and watch. Some of them are even a good source of encouragement to the players that have been chosen to be in the game.

The Christian church is like this football team. We have a small number of people who play every game. They are always busy in ministry or evangelism for the leader (owner) of our team, who is Jesus Christ. We have another group that represents the second team. They provide the backup support each team needs. They are our prayer warriors, fulfilling a vital role on our team. When needed, or asked, they jump in the "game" with the first team and play very well.

A larger number of us just ride the bench. There is very little hope that we will ever be playing in the game, because although we have chosen to be on the team, we lack the desire or passion to perform as well as the chosen players. We lack commitment. We don't have the confidence it takes to excel. It is okay with us if we sit on the bench. We are still recognized as part of the team and will share the joy when we win and the sadness when we lose. We are team members!

The majority of us, however, are part of that twelfth man. We are the fans! At our local stadium, the fans comprise approximately 80,000 members while the team on the field may be only 80. So the fans are 1,000 times the total number of players, and 2,000 times the number of players that actually participate on game day. To further compare these numbers with participating church membership would lead to astronomical results and be unproductive.

Being a Christian disciple means that we don't consider our faith to be the equivalent of a spectator sport. If our life is anything less than complete obedience with a personal, passionate relationship with Jesus Christ, then we are living beneath our privilege and potential as a forgiven soldier of the cross. A Christian disciple will honor his God with obedience, service, and ministry while enjoying the fruit of his or her salvation. We want to be on the first team of Christ!

The question is: where are you on this Christian team? Are you a first-team player? Second team? Perhaps you are relegated to the bench? If so, do you encourage those who are playing? Or, are you a twelfth man – a spectator in the stands?

God doesn't have any "best" players. He wants to use every one of us! He has equipped us specifically for the team work that lies before us. Remember, *"the harvest is abundant, but the workers are few"* (Matt. 9:37).

The workers are few because most of us choose to be disobedient to His word that commands us to ministry and evangelism. It appears we would rather watch others build up our church, minister to others, or evangelize.

According to the Barna network, LifeWay Research, and other credible research firms, less than 20% of church membership performs over 80% of the work. Of course, this is not true in every church, but across the board the numbers are real: almost 90% of self-proclaimed Christians choose not to be involved in any type of ministry or evangelism. These numbers are staggering! Who are these people? We are laity! We are the laypeople who join the church for our own reasons and not God's reasons. We attend church for our purpose and not specifically to worship a living God and His Son, Jesus Christ. We have subliminally chosen to be disobedient!

Don't ask us to work. It is sufficient for us to attend church and occasionally donate money to help with church projects or to help other people. Isn't that the way we football fans support our team? We attend games when we can and spend inordinate amounts of money to show our support for the team. We have no intention to ever "suit up" for the game. Often we will encourage the active team (other laity and church staff) to do well. We are content!

Where is our passion for Christ? Has He not given us a passion? Well, yes, He has. If you don't feel the passion, you have allowed other priorities to enter your life that consume the passions of your heart. *"For where your treasure is, there your heart will be also"* (Matt. 6:21). These are the words of Jesus Christ. He made us and He sees us for who and what we really are. He knows that we have other priorities. He simply asks us to be obedient and arrange our priorities so that we are living a lifestyle of ministry and evangelism. Why? To grow the Kingdom of God.

God so loved us enough to send His son Jesus to earth to become a living sacrifice for all of us who choose to believe. We don't want to be obedient just because He commands us to obey. We should want to be obedient because of the great love He has shown to us. He showed us this love not just to let us join Him in heaven, but to reconcile us to Him to love Him, praise Him, and worship Him. We can never love Him enough to pay back the love He has shown for us, but we can be obedient to His commands and use our passion for the purpose for which God saved us in the first place.

If we find our passion, we will find our purpose. I encourage you to pray that you will let the passion that God has put into your heart to come to the surface. God does not fail and He will not let you fail either. He has given you the passion, the gift, the purpose, and the tools to succeed. You can move from the stands to the field and to the first team. The choice is yours. God has equipped you for the purpose He wants you to see.

Show your trust in Him by accepting the challenge of purpose that He has given to you. You will be a winner! And forever you will hear the accolades and cheers of all heavenly inhabitants.

Questions for Self-Examination:

1. *Do you attend church regularly and participate in its activities?*

2. *Have you shown a willingness to be involved in ministry or evangelism events?*

3. *Do you actively demonstrate that you are a Christian beyond the walls of the church?*

4. *Do others see God's purpose for you being played out in your life?*

5. *Does your purpose for serving match your passion?*

6. *Do you strive to be on the first team in your church?*

Your answers to these questions should lead you to a time of personal prayer, meditation, and Bible study. Seek God's guidance as you question your involvement in ministry or evangelism. Ask God to forgive you for your disobedience and to lead you to His purpose for your life.

God's purpose in redeeming men from sin is not to give them freedom to do as they please but freedom to do as He pleases, which is to live righteously.

John F. McArthur, evangelical writer and minister

The purpose of the Bible is to proclaim God's plan and passion to save His children.

Max Lucado, author, pastor, lecturer

Chapter 3

AN OVERVIEW OF THE SPIRITUAL LIFE JOURNEY

For it is God who is working in you, enabling you both to will and to act for His good purpose.

Philippians 2:13

When thinking about how to define our spiritual journey, some put an emphasis on the visible events of our life, defining this journey as our encounters with whatever comes our way. But I view our spiritual journey as our personal walk with God, always seeking to draw closer to Him to fulfill His plan of reconciliation. It is a journey that begins with salvation and continues through eternity with God, and our progress is often invisible to the world's eyes. Notice that the cross of Jesus Christ is at the center of our journey, as He is to be the center of our life. As we progress through the four stages of this journey, we discover our passion and purpose to serve Jesus Christ as He intended when He called us unto salvation, and it culminates in a lifestyle of ministry and evangelism. In this chapter, we will work our way through the four stages of this journey on our way to eternity with our heavenly Father.

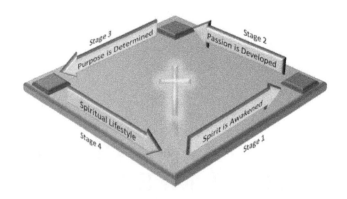

Figure 1. The four stages of our Spiritual Life Journey.

(Note: No home plate is pictured, as there is no end to this journey except in heaven.)

Stage One: Our Spirit Is Awakened

We begin our journey in the first stage by moving to "first base." This is our spiritual awakening. At this time in our life, we come to the conclusion that we need Jesus; we accept Him into our life and are awarded the grace gift of salvation for an eternity. The very words of Jesus the Christ reveal this truth: *"I am the way, the truth, and the life. No one comes to the Father except through me"* (John 14:6). He is our doorkeeper. If we want to enter the Kingdom of Heaven, we must accept that Jesus Christ is the Son of God; He died on the cross as a propitiation for our sin. God raised Him from among the dead and gave Him authority over all things in heaven and on earth.

This awakening of the spirit within us causes an innate desire to join a church and be baptized. The first stage of our journey has begun. Unfortunately, for many of us, we accept the gift of salvation, move to first base, then stay there for the rest of our life. *That's not what God wants for us!* He wants us to give the gift of ourselves back to Him. As we progress around the bases with the ultimate goal of achieving a spiritual lifestyle, we will learn how God wants us to do this.

Our spiritual awakening comes at a time in our life when we finally realize that we can't travel this sphere alone. We need someone who can provide inner strength that will help us overcome the many trials that will come our way—education, job security, illness, relationships, even death. We move spiritually from an apostate lifestyle to one of heavenly peace and everything changes. Our demeanor changes, our language changes, our compassion for others grows and our heart reaches out to God daily. We even discover a passion for God that can't be suppressed. We can't wait to tell others of the new-found joy we are experiencing. Remember how excited you were when you first accepted Christ? You couldn't wait to tell your family, your friends, even some strangers. Your passion was that strong.

We all have the passion given to us by God himself, but many have suppressed it. So what happened? Somewhere along the way, we became complacent. We now may believe that attending church on Sunday morning is all we need to do to return God's grace gift to Him. Our passion is waning. We have not found a purpose for our own Christianity. We are stuck on the first base of our journey. We have staked out our favorite pew in the neighborhood church. Some of us have even volunteered to usher or sing in the choir. Once in a while we will serve on a committee as long as we aren't asked to do so often. Others of us attend Sunday School on a regular basis. But please, don't ask us to prayer walk, go on missions, or get spiritually involved in our neighborhood, school, or business!

Where is our first Love? Where is the excitement that we once showed to our family and friends when Jesus came into our life? Along with this complacency, we see a return to loneliness and a hardening of our compassion for others. We are not satisfied with our own spirituality. Yet we don't seem to understand this change or how to go back to our time of excitement, compassion, and peace. But Jesus has the answer: *"Repent, and do the works you did at first"* (Rev. 2:5b).

This is a spiritual problem. It can be caused by either our willful disobedience to the will of God, or perhaps we have turned to material substitutes for God's love and peace. But the church also needs to accept partial blame for this complacency. For the church often is more concerned about the number of members in attendance than the number of members in ministry. Too many churches today don't preach, teach, or encourage their membership to go beyond the walls of the church into a ministry as God intended.

The late Dr. Findley Edge, former professor at Southern Baptist Theological Seminary, once made the profound statement that *"the problem in today's church is not the empty pews but the empty people sitting in them."* Undoubtedly, Dr. Edge was referring to the church spectators we discussed in chapter 2. The solution appears to be that we may need to quit sitting on our hands watching Christianity unfold, and begin actively participating in the advancement of His Kingdom here on earth.

If we are to replace this empty, complacent lifestyle with one that is spiritually fulfilling, we must be willing to move along on our journey to find the passion and purpose that will lead us to a lifestyle of ministry and evangelism. We need to increase our level of obedience to the commands of our God and progress through this Spiritual Life Journey. Begin by moving from Stage One to Stage Two, in search of the passion that will lead us to the purpose for which we have been saved.

Stage Two: Our Passion Is Ignited

For those of us who do attend church regularly and get involved in its teachings, i.e., Sunday School, discipleship training, Bible study, and prayer, movement towards the second base of our journey beckons. Serious Christians begin to feel a need to be more involved and to reach out to others with compassion, mercy, and understanding. What is driving this feeling? The passion that Christ put into our being when we first accepted Him into our life may be cracking the shell of its suppressed state. We have had this passion all along, having received it as a gift from the Holy Spirit when we first accepted Christ, but most of us do a pretty good job of suppressing it and keeping it hidden beneath our superficial surface.

In Stage Two, the teaching of God's word through the various programs of our church begins to have an effect. This is the equipping, or teaching, of the saints that Paul is referring to in his letter to the Ephesians: *"He personally gave some to be apostles, some prophets, some evangelists, some pastors and teachers, for the training of the saints in the work of ministry"* (Eph. 4:11-12). The purpose of the training and equipping of the saints is to *"build up the body of Christ, until we all reach unity in the faith and in the knowledge of God's Son"* (v. 13a).

Our suppressed passion is being ignited and we have a burning desire to learn more and to begin practicing the principles of service to others that we are now learning. We begin to develop habits that lead to greater spiritual maturity. Complacency and the apostate lifestyle of our past begin to disappear. We're developing a personal relationship with Jesus Christ through more fervent prayer and intensified Bible study. New daily habits of discipleship allow us to walk *with* Jesus and not just towards Him.

Our friends notice we are spending more time at church. Our pastor rejoices as our passion leads us to become more active in church activities. We thrive on helping others to draw closer to Christ. We begin looking outside the church for additional ways to serve the needs of others. Friends and neighbors are being invited to church. Like newlyweds with a new lover, our passion grows and we look for ways to satisfy this burning desire to please God and share His Son with others. The second base of our journey is now in sight.

Along the way we learn that fellowship with Christ must come before service for Christ. We realize that God's not responsible for maintaining our passion. We are! God has placed a passion for service in all of us as a gift. We now own it and can either accept it or reject it. As we continue along the spiritual path towards the second base of our journey, we also learn that we had long been hiding our passion from our own view. Now God has re-ignited this passion within us. We accept it!

At the same time, some of this passion is extended to the church as others witness our excitement and commitment. Passion is contagious, and the church begins to see membership increasing and a new spiritual growth among its members. We are joined by others who feel their own passion leading them to reach out with compassion and service. Please, please church: do not discourage this contagious spread of passion for service.

We are no longer uncomfortable with our service because our comfort zone has expanded as God planned. A new joy is found in helping others that becomes our reward. Friends see the "fruit of the Spirit" coming to fruition in us. A few of our courageous friends ask how our life has changed. We see this as an excellent opportunity to testify about the passion that has been ignited in us.

Unfortunately, too many of our fellow church members never move beyond the first stage of this spiritual journey. While they may admire our growing passion for ministry, they seem to be ambivalent and content right where they are – sitting in their favorite pew. We pray for them too, that they may have their passion ignited so they can join us in ministry and service. But we press on towards the mark, and the third stage of our spiritual life journey: purpose.

Stage Three: Our Purpose Is Determined

Now that our passion has been ignited, the question becomes, "What will we do with it?" For me, I felt almost hyperactive. I was excitedly jumping up and down looking for ways to serve so this passion could be released. I couldn't just sit still at the second base of this journey. I was compelled to continue walking with Jesus in search of the purpose for which I was called.

I admit that all Christians may not feel this same level of excitement when their passion is ignited. Nevertheless, they will know that their passion has been ignited and it will be difficult to contain. In Part Two, you'll read how a few biblical characters released their passion in the purpose for which God called them.

The important thing is to release the passion within you and channel it to a specific ministry. It could be either within your church or outside your church walls. It could be in your neighborhood, business, school, or even in another country. God has a plan for you and will let you know where you can serve Him with passion. Ask and listen!

One of the first actions I took when I realized that I had a newfound passion that needed to be directed towards a specific purpose was to pray the prayer of Jabez. *"Jabez called out to the God of Israel: 'If only You would bless me, extend my border, let Your hand be with me, and keep me from harm, so that I will not cause any pain.' And God granted his request"* (1 Chron. 4:10).

Much has been written about the wording of this prayer. But when I prayed, I simply asked God to expand the mission field where I could best use the spiritual gift that He gave to me when I accepted Christ. You may not pray the prayer of Jabez as I did, but certainly you should pray in some manner that God will direct your passion to His purpose.

He assuredly answered me! In addition to teaching Sunday School, I began to also teach mid-week Bible study, lead men's ministry, and even joined the nationwide ministry of lay renewal. Yet I felt that God did not give me more to do than His gift would allow, nor did I ever feel overworked.

God had a plan for me and He has a plan for you. He will never give you more than you can handle. He will never give you so much work that you might neglect your family. He has called you. He has gifted you. He has equipped you. He has sent you. If you can admit these four points, you are well on your way to achieving a lifestyle of ministry and evangelism.

By this time on your journey, you should already have developed good habits of prayer and Bible study. Remember, Jesus asked us to take up our cross daily, not just once in a while. In Psalm 34, David confesses that he will praise the Lord at all times. Christ expects this frequency from all of us.

With good praise and worship habits now established, we should become very proactive in discovering our spiritual gift, developing it, and finding ways to use it with passion. It is imperative that you discover your spiritual gift in this stage of your journey, as this gift will lead you to the purpose for which God has called you.

There are many ways to determine your spiritual gift. I encourage you to use the appropriate material from the reading list in Appendix C and begin the process, if you don't already know what your gift is. You may also check with your church or nearby bookstore for other resources that are available.

Please note that there is a multitude of books available on the subject of spiritual gifts. Some lists identify as many as thirty different gifts, and even include as gifts those qualities that Paul calls fruits of the spirit. Other lists include the nine gifts of manifestation contained in chapter 12 of Paul's first letter to the Corinthians. Still other lists include positions rather than gifts, i.e., pastors, apostles, prophets, etc. In order for you to effectively use your gift for a long-term ministry, I encourage you to concentrate on the seven motivational gifts Paul listed in chapter 12 of his letter to the Romans: *"According to the grace given to us, we have different gifts: If **prophecy**, use it according to the standard of faith; if **service**, in service; if **teaching**, in teaching; if **exhorting**, in exhortation; **giving**, with generosity; **leading**, with diligence; showing **mercy**, with cheerfulness."*

These appear to be the gifts that motivate us towards a specific ministry where we can serve God's purpose with passion. And that is our goal in Stage Three. One or more of these gifts has been given to you. They are permanent, irrevocable, and given to us without choice. I encourage you to follow the lead of the Holy Spirit and you will be led to the appropriate gift that God purposed for you. As you continue to study and learn about your spiritual gift, the more ways you will find to discover that gift and its usefulness in ministry. If you have been given more than one gift, the stronger will be used in the primary ministry God has purposed for you and the other will be used in a secondary ministry.

When God gave one, or more, of those spiritual gifts to you, He gave the gift that best uses the abilities, personality, and experiences that He brought into your life for such a time as this. That is the equipping phase of God's gift to you. He has called you by name, He has given to you a motivational spiritual gift, He has equipped you over time to use the gift, and now He is sending you into a mission field where you can serve Him with great passion.

If this sounds simple, it really is. You are in Stage Three of the Spiritual Life Journey. All you need to do is acknowledge that God has saved you for a specific purpose, be willing to step out of the darkness into the light of His world, and serve Him according to His plan. Your spiritual gift is there before you, and He is waiting for you to take up your cross and follow. There is no greater means of using your passion than to show your good works through the spiritual gift for which He has purposed you.

Stage Four: A Lifestyle of Ministry and Evangelism Is Achieved

By now you should be feeling the passion and excitement within you as you pursue the great purpose that God intended for your life. You are embarking on the final stage of your spiritual journey on earth. Experiencing the passion and using it to further God's Kingdom with your chosen purpose does not complete the journey, however. A lifestyle change is needed.

Achieving a goal of developing and maintaining a lifestyle of ministry and evangelism should be the ambition of all Christians. It is quite possible that God's chosen purpose for you may not be in the area of evangelism. Yet evangelism is part of the journey because we are commanded to evangelize nonbelievers. God has a plan of redemption for all mankind, and He needs our help to accomplish His plan.

Let's review these commands. The Great Commission is perhaps the most remembered of all the commissioning commands: *"Go, therefore, and make disciples of all nations, baptizing them in the name of the Father and of the Son and of the Holy Spirit, teaching them to observe everything I have commanded you"* (Matt. 28:19-20a). In order to make people disciples, we must first help them to understand who Jesus is and why they, and we, need Him as a Savior. This is our evangelism as we advocate the Gospel of Jesus Christ.

Dr. Luke recorded this command in the Acts of the Apostles: *"But you will receive power when the Holy Spirit comes upon you, and you will be My witnesses in Jerusalem, in all Judea and Samaria, and to the ends of the earth"* (Acts 1:8). To be His witness is to evangelize others, and He excluded no one person, family, tribe, or country.

Another lesser known command is *"Go into all the world and preach the gospel to the whole creation"* (Mark 16:15). And when John recorded Jesus' command to Peter, *"Feed My sheep"* (John 21:17c), I believe He was speaking to all of us who believe. The Holy Word of God is very consistent in describing God's plan of salvation for all mankind, as are His commands for us to join Him in ministry and evangelism to accomplish His plan of reconciliation.

In this fourth stage of our journey, we realize that our lifestyle should reflect our love for Him and our passionate desire to help build up His Kingdom here on earth. It goes beyond just finding a suitable ministry in accordance with our grace gift from God (Stage Three). It means we should also look for and act upon those challenges and opportunities that God puts before us daily to reconcile others to Him.

At this point, we should note that God did not, and does not, call everyone to be a pastor, teacher, or deacon, but everyone *is* called to be a minister and evangelist. I have been given the spiritual gift of teaching with a secondary gift of leadership. Yet I know that I am called upon to evangelize the lost and minister to others as the need, or opportunity, arises.

A short time ago, my wife and I visited a retail store and asked for assistance with a purchase. The young lady who was sent to help us appeared to have a cold as she had tearful eyes, a sniffling nose, and not very good concentration. As our conversation progressed, it became apparent to me that she was not ill, but emotionally distraught. I knew that God had placed her before us this day, but I was wary. After all, doesn't God know that I weaken when confronted with tearful young ladies? Even so, He gave me the courage to ask if she had an issue that we could pray about.

That question opened the floodgates, and she told us that just before we walked in the door, her doctor called and confirmed that she had miscarried over the weekend—for the third time! We gathered this young lady to us, wrapped our arms around her, and just prayed for God to place His hand of grace upon her. This was very comforting to her, and a lesson for us.

I learned that, aside from the motivational gifts listed by Paul in Romans 12, we are provided with gifts that are a manifestation of the Spirit when necessary to produce what is beneficial to others. (See Paul's list of these gifts in I Cor. 12.) The motivational gift(s) appears to be permanent, while a gift of manifestation may be provided to us temporarily when God challenges us with an opportunity to minister or evangelize. In the circumstance I just described, God temporarily gave me the gifts of wisdom and encouragement that I normally do not exhibit. This is more confirmation that God will always equip us for any situation He presents before us to act upon. We no longer need to fear. He is always with us to guide us, to challenge us, and to equip us for every good work in His name. Once we use the gift in response to the opportunity given to us, this temporary gift may be returned to the Holy Spirit until it is needed again. We should always be ready to meet the challenges and opportunities put before us with the assurance that the proper gift will be given to us to minister to the needs of others when necessary.

A spiritual lifestyle of ministry and evangelism is achieved in Stage Four when we are actively serving with passion and purpose while sharing the gospel of Jesus Christ with others. God has chosen us, He has sent us, He challenges us, He equips us, and He expects us to deliver. The question is: Do we love Him enough to answer the call?

I encourage you to say yes and feel the overpowering joy that only He can provide when we agree to serve with Him in His mission field.

Now that we've seen an overview of the four stages of the Spiritual Life Journey, we'll take a look at some common issues that arise in each stage.

A call to salvation is a call to be on mission with our Lord. This call was not just for a select few but to all who were called to a relationship with Christ.

Henry Blackaby, author, speaker, pastor

Is it not a sad thing that after all Christ's love to us, we should repay it with lukewarm love to Him?

Charles H. Spurgeon, author and preacher

Chapter 4

WHO IS JESUS?

Therefore, everyone who will acknowledge Me before men, I will also acknowledge him before My Father in heaven.

Matthew 10:32

As we begin Stage One, and before we can bring out our passion and apply it to the purpose for which God saved us, we must have a right relationship with Jesus Christ. He is the foundation of our faith and the one for whom we must develop a lifestyle of ministry and evangelism. Jesus told us, *"I am the way, the truth, and the life. No one comes to the Father except through me"* (John 14:6).

First of all, we need to answer for ourselves, who is Jesus? Is He your friend, your Savior, your Lord, a prophet? How does He affect your life? What is your priority for Jesus?

When Jesus walked this earth, He knew who He was and where His walk was leading him. He was the Son of Man, the Messiah! However, calling Jesus "the Christ" or "God's son" was a criminal offense. Either of these statements could lead to a death sentence and did in many cases. The Jewish and Roman leaders persecuted Christians who took a stand for their faith. His closest disciples, who walked with Him daily, were even cautious about publicly admitting who He really was. It was just too risky!

In this environment, the disciples looked away and grew fearful when Jesus proclaimed that He was the Son of Man. They were afraid to admit their own faith. Yet Jesus gathered this stunned, scared group around Him for a final teaching. No one wanted to make eye contact with him. There was total silence.

Jesus asked, *"Who do people say that the Son of Man is?"* (Matt. 16:13). They gave every answer but the right one. They were simply too afraid to utter the truth. *"But you, who do you say that I am?"* (16:15). You know it had to be Peter who spoke first. He was the leader, the impetuous one with strange courage. As if he finally understood, Peter looked Jesus right in the eye and declared, *"You are the Messiah, the Son of the living God"* (16:16). He finally got it right!

Our church today has just the opposite problem. We are quick to proclaim "Jesus is Lord!" But too many of us fail to go about His work and ministry. Like the disciples long ago, we prefer to remain silent. Sure, we may be persecuted for our belief, but nothing like it was just over 2,000 years ago. On Sunday we sing, "I love to tell the story," but the rest of the week, we love to be silent and not share this wonderful news that we feel has saved us from an eternity in hell.

Consider what you so willingly share on Sunday at church with the professions of your mouth. Now what do you do for the Kingdom? Jesus calls us to be complete in both testimony and deed wherever we are. If we confess that "Jesus is Lord," then shouldn't our life reflect that declaration? I encourage you to begin to share both your testimony and your good works with others so that they may see your faith.

Paul reminds us that *"You yourselves are our letter, written on our hearts, recognized and read by everyone"* (2 Cor. 3:2). Many may know that you are a Christian, but have they heard your testimony? Do they see your good work? If we are a living letter recognized and read by everyone, our lives should reflect our faith 24/7. We can't help others come to Christ if they don't see us living out our faith. Our faith can't have two sides to it. It must be fully expressed in Jesus Christ. It must be shared with others. It must be an example that others will see so that they have a desire to join the family of Christ. This is our passion being expressed for the One who gave us that passion.

Once we identify Jesus as our Lord and Savior, we can begin to develop a lifestyle of ministry and evangelism. Answer the question: who is Jesus? With the right answer firmly planted in your heart, the passion that He has placed there also will be revealed to you. If Jesus is in your heart, shouldn't He be in your life also? Please believe that it's okay to let others see Him in you.

After all, most Americans have already admitted that they are Christians. Granted there is considerable variation in what that means to most believers. One thing is certain. The Christian today is expected to lead a good life. But if Christ is your Savior, your good life will become a great life in Him. The passion will surface and you will find the purpose for which He has given you the free gift of salvation.

It is up to us laity to find our passion, release it, and let the purpose of our belief unfold. The harvest is ready and the fields are plentiful. Let's allow ourselves to be renewed so we can begin sharing our faith. Although there may be millions of people already in heaven, there is room for more. God doesn't want us to come to Him empty-handed. He wants us to bring with us as many believers as we can.

We need not worry about who God chooses for His Kingdom. He has told us that *all* who believe shall have an eternity with Him. He will find the ones He wants, He will put them in front of you, and He will give you the courage and the words to speak. We never have to do this alone! God is always with us, guiding us, preparing us, and lighting our paths. Jesus told us that we would receive power when the Holy Spirit comes upon us (Acts 1:8). We have the power of God in us! That should be the only impetus we need to serve with passion and purpose.

Questions for Self-Examination

1. *Do you believe in Jesus Christ or do you KNOW Jesus Christ?*

2. *Have you developed a personal relationship with Jesus Christ?*

3. *Do you commune with Him daily through prayer?*

4. *Have your family and friends heard your testimony?*

A "no" answer to any of the above questions will indicate a need for additional prayer and Bible study. Being active in ministry provides a great opportunity to practice giving your testimony in front of other believers. Then, when the opportunity to testify to nonbelievers arises, you can speak with greater confidence.

You're through. Finished. Burned out. Used up. You've been replaced, forgotten. That's a lie!

Charles R. Swindoll, author, speaker, pastor

God is seeking to develop the character of His Son Jesus in each of us. This is His eternal purpose. He would do through our lives what He was able to do through His Son.

Henry Blackaby, author, speaker, pastor

Chapter 5

IS JESUS YOUR FRIEND?

> *If you continue in My word, you really are My disciples. You will know the truth, and the truth will set you free.*

John 8:31-32

A few years ago, E.D. Hill wrote a book entitled, *I'm Not Your Friend, I'm Your Parent.* That simple title revealed to me that too often we see Jesus as our friend. But is He our friend? In a sense, He certainly is our friend. Yet as we come to know Jesus in Stage One and beyond, we realize that Jesus Christ is so much more than our friend. Friends can be disappointing at times. Jesus never is! Friends can break a promise. Jesus never does! Friends don't walk each step of our life with us. Jesus always does!

Consider John the disciple. He leads us to believe that he was the disciple *"whom Jesus loved"* (John 13:23), yet with all of John's belief that Jesus was his friend, he couldn't face our Savior in all of His glory. John was so committed to Jesus' friendship and teaching, and his gospel of love aptly shows how much he loved Jesus. Now, fast forward a few decades after Jesus' ascension. John is taken up to heaven to witness and record the revelation of Jesus Christ that God gave Him to show to John.

John records that he was in the Spirit when he heard a loud voice behind him. He turned to see the voice that was speaking. Try to envision what John saw: *"seven gold lampstands, and among the lampstands was One like the Son of Man, dressed in a long robe, and with a gold sash wrapped around His chest. His head and hair were white like wool—white as snow, His eyes like a fiery flame, His feet like fine bronze fired in a furnace, and His voice like the sound of cascading waters. In His right hand He had seven stars; from His mouth came a sharp two-edged sword; and His face was shining like the sun at midday"* (Rev. 1:12-16).

John further records, *"When I saw Him, I fell at His feet like a dead man"* (Rev. 1:17). Did John see his friend? No! He saw our everlasting Lord and Savior in Jesus Christ. While Jesus wants us to love Him intimately as a friend, we should never forget who He is nor should we ever make Him less than who He really is. We should reverently love Him and reverently obey Him in all contexts.

Jesus is much more than our friend. He is our living, loving God! You have never had a friend like this—He loves you all the time. Everything He does is for your benefit—to draw you closer to Him. He receives the glory, but we receive the benefit. Friends are special for sure, but nothing like this friend.

Yet we often treat him as even less than a friend. We go to church and sing, "What a Friend We Have in Jesus," but how often are we willing to share this "friend" with others? Shouldn't we introduce our "friend" to others and explain why this friend is so special? Jesus wants us to tell others. He wants us to speak with Him daily. He wants us to bring our grief, sorrows, joy, and disappointments to Him so He can repair the hurts or rejoice with us.

He has given us a passion for a specific purpose. That passion is the overwhelming desire to please Him with our love for others by demonstrating an innate zeal for ministry and evangelism. It is the result of acknowledging His great sacrificial love for us when He willingly went to the cross as a propitiation for our sin debt to God. That passion is within all of us, but it may be suppressed in favor of the material desires of our life or fear of ridicule. If we release these inhibitions, we will find our passion and purpose for serving that will allow us to draw closer to Him and really be His friend. An earnest prayer life will help us get past these roadblocks as we seek to draw closer to the One who saved us. More discussion of this process can be found in chapter 8. It all begins with a personal relationship with Jesus. We must be willing to give Him all that we are so that He can make us to be all that we can be.

Our spiritual life has to be more than just about salvation. God didn't save us just for a trip to heaven. He saved us for a specific purpose. That purpose is to grow His Kingdom. We do that by committing ourselves to a lifestyle of ministry and evangelism. Would you do anything less for your best friend?

Ignorance has caused humanity more harm than anything else on earth.

Jack Hatfield, author

God calls you to partner with Him in a mission that is bigger than you are.

Bob Record, author, speaker, NAMB past president

Chapter 6

SPIRITUAL PASSION

Guard your heart above all else, for it is the source of life.

Proverbs 4:23

Several dictionaries define "passion" as a powerful emotion coupled with boundless enthusiasm. This is the definition that we will use as we enter Stage Two, because we want to determine what it is about our spirituality that causes us to have an enthusiastic, strong, positive emotion for serving Jesus Christ. Passion transcends love, with a stronger personal desire for a person, object, or purpose. Often this passion is uncontrollable or irresistible because it originates in the heart. Spiritually, the only way we can feel complete is to respond positively to the passion that is driving us towards the specific purpose that God intended for us when we were created in our mother's womb. When we do not respond favorably, guilt sets in and we become complacent and discouraged. This is how we can lose our passion and purpose for loving and serving our living God.

But the Lord said to Samuel, *"Do not look at his appearance or his stature, because I have rejected him. Man does not see what the Lord sees, for man sees what is visible, but the Lord sees the heart"* (1 Sam. 16:7).

God knows what is in our heart, the good along with the bad. He also knows what drives us to serve or what drives us not to be obedient to His will. Scripture tells us that the heart is the source of life. It is here that our emotions are formed. Some emotions are good, and some are bad for us. Our spirituality may well be dictated by the stronger passions that fill our heart. Jesus said, *"For where your treasure is, there your heart will be also"* (Matt. 6:21).

Of course, we want our passion (emotions) to be positive towards the spirituality that our mind thinks is right. But that doesn't always happen, does it? If it did, we would have the passion and purpose that we need to be obedient to the commands of our God. Too often, though, worldviews or distractions become roadblocks to fulfilling our calling.

Our heart, as the source of our passion and emotions, can either prompt us to ministry or allow worldly distractions to keep us from moving off that comfortable pew. The key is to have a heart (passion) to become more like Christ. When you have the passion for Christ that leads to finding a purpose in serving Him, then you are well on your way to developing and maintaining a lifestyle of ministry and evangelism. Isn't that really what Christ has called us to do?

My friend Dale had a passion for evangelism. He would take his wife to the local shopping mall where she could stroll around the mall and shop. He was unable to accompany her because of his health. So she always deposited Dale in the sitting area close to the center of the mall. This always seemed to be a place for men to congregate while their wives shopped. If you sat near Dale, he immediately began a dialogue about faith. I learned of this ministry when I went to the mall during a lunch break and found him sitting with other men in the waiting area. It did not surprise me to find them in a discussion of the Bible.

I learned from Dale that when other men sat near him, he initiated a conversation by asking, "What church do you attend?" If they answered with a church name, then an open discussion of the Bible followed. If they replied that they were "in between churches," or did not attend at all, then Dale opened with his own witness to the power of Jesus Christ. I watched Dale on several occasions and was even invited to join the discussions on a regular basis. Now, I'm not an evangelist, but I love the Lord. It was not difficult to work with Dale to help others understand who Jesus was and how He could bring peace to their lives. While he was serving God in evangelism, he was also encouraging me to be more useful by finding a stronger purpose for my life. That's how ministry works. One worker encourages another, who encourages another, and so on.

Spiritual passion is a grace gift from God and is given to each believer at the time of our repentance and acceptance of Jesus Christ as our Savior. But remember, although God has placed a passion for service within each of us, He does not own it. We own it and can either accept it or reject it.

My friend Dale had a passion for loving Christ and sharing the good news with others. He used that passion to find a purpose that fit his lifestyle. I called it Dale's mall ministry. I am so proud of Dale for finding a way to use his gift and his passion in a purposeful way to serve the Lord he loves so much.

I know that when God reached down to save me, He gifted me and gave me a passion for teaching others. After a while, a purpose was put in my soul to reach out to other laity to help them develop and maintain a lifestyle of ministry and evangelism. It is, as Paul states it in his letter to the Ephesians, *"for the training of the saints in the work of ministry, to build up the body of Christ, until we all reach unity in the faith"* (Eph. 4:12-13).

I didn't always have the passion and purpose that I now enjoy. It was suppressed by my desire to do good works and be recognized by others for my ministry. I now know that was the wrong approach. I needed to put aside the driving force for personal recognition and allow the passion that was placed in my heart to come forward and control my life. It took a while, but I feel stronger in my faith as I allow the Lord to use me in various ways as He has given me a passion and a purpose to carry on and help others.

That purpose is to help other laypeople to step up to their calling and not be afraid to release their own passion for serving Jesus Christ. That old adage that 80% of the work is done by 20% of the workers is still true. In some churches, those numbers are 90% and 10% respectively. That very well may be the cause of the declining or plateauing membership of so many of our churches nationwide.

We laypeople have become so comfortable in our pews that we just can't stand up and release the passion and purpose that God has put in each of us. From where does this hesitancy come? Do we perceive ridicule if we get involved? Do we feel that we are not qualified to serve? Or could it be that we are indeed just lukewarm as previously discussed? I believe it's a test of our faith. God has equipped us for whatever purpose He intended, so if we choose not to become involved, our faith may need to be strengthened so that we can serve Him as He commanded.

For example, some of us appear to be passionate for the Word of God but not passionate about serving Him with a lifestyle of ministry and evangelism. Now I don't advocate good works as the way to get to heaven. We are saved by grace! Nevertheless, James tells us that faith without works is dead (James 2:17).

Dr. Adrian Rogers once said, *"We are justified before God by faith; and justified before men by works."* By our faith we work so that others may see us as true believers. Not for selfish reasons, but for God's glory!

Too many of us may be just lukewarm in our passion for Jesus Christ. But that's not good enough for Him. We need to be on fire for Him in our worship, our praise, our study, and our service to others. After saying that faith without works is dead, James goes on to say, *"Show me your faith without works, and I will show you faith from my works"* (James 2:18). If we are not showing our faith by our works, how can we demonstrate to others that we are Christians?

Too often, we Christians are called hypocrites by nonbelievers. Likely this is precisely because our works don't match our beliefs. How can we change that? We can get out of the pews and find a ministry where we can use our God-given passion for the specific purpose to which He has called us.

The Apostle Paul explained in his letter to Titus that Jesus gave Himself up for us, *"that He might redeem us from every lawless deed and purify for Himself His own special people, zealous for good works."* (Titus 2:14)

I believe that every Christian individually and every church corporately must have a burning, passionate, emotional love for the Lord Jesus Christ that overflows in service and worship to Him. Without spiritual passion and purpose in our life, we may be destined to a life of mediocrity.

My encouragement to the reader is to turn your passion into a purpose that will lead to a ministry that brings glory to our Heavenly Father. Believe what is written in Philippians 2:13: *"For it is God who is working in you, enabling you both to will and to act for His good purpose."* When we act for His good purpose, then our purpose becomes His purpose and we have presented our *"bodies as a living sacrifice, holy, and pleasing to God"* (Rom. 12:1).

Questions for Self-Examination

1. *Do you have an enthusiastic, emotional drive for serving in ministry? Have you responded to this passion?*

2. *Do you question your obedience to His command for ministry and evangelism?*

3. *Are your priorities purpose driven?*

4. *Do you feel God leading you in a specific direction?*

Your answers to these questions should lead you to committed, interactive prayer to focus on the things God wants you to do, even if it's out of your comfort zone.

More men fail through lack of purpose than lack of talent.

Billy Sunday, American evangelist

In Christ alone, and His payment of the penalty for our sins upon the Cross, we find reconciliation to God and ultimate meaning and purpose.

Dave Hunt, Christian apologist and speaker

Chapter 7

GOD'S GREAT PURPOSE

*We know that all things work together for the good
of those who love God: those who are called according
to His purpose.*

Romans 8:28

One of the greatest joys of the Christian life is to know
and be obedient to the purpose that God has planned for us.
God doesn't save us so we can be a spectator to His great
works, nor does He expect us to spend our Christian life
sitting in a pew and singing songs of praise and worship that
may never take us beyond the walls of our church sanctuary.
No, He saves us for a specific purpose and He always reveals
that purpose to us. As we enter Stage Three, we enter this joy.

Henry Blackaby, noted author, pastor, and speaker, once
said, *"God is not pleased if you praise Him at church but
not at your workplace. It is not acceptable for you to revere
God when you are with other Christians, but not in your
community, workplace, or school. He expects you to honor
Him completely, all the time, with your words, with your
actions, with your life."*

We must learn to take the passion that God has given to us and direct that passion towards a useful purpose that He has revealed to us. God never keeps His purpose for us a secret. As you read through the Scriptures, you will find that in every instance where God chose someone to implement His purpose, He revealed that purpose to the chosen servant. And Jesus did the same thing when He met Paul on the road to Damascus; He made His purpose known through Ananias: *"this man [Paul] is My chosen instrument to carry My name before Gentiles, kings, and the sons of Israel"* (Acts 9:15).

To Moses, God said, *"Go. I am sending you to Pharaoh so that you may lead My people, the Israelites, out of Egypt"* (Exod. 3:10).

God sent Samuel to anoint David as the successor to Saul as the King of Israel. God told Joshua that he was to lead the people to cross over the Jordan River to the Promised Land. These are only a few examples of God's sharing plan that are revealed in His Holy Word.

God has a purpose for each person who accepts Jesus Christ as Savior, and He will reveal His purpose for you at the right time. If you do not know the purpose for which God has chosen you for salvation, it could be that you have not been attentive to His calling.

We know that we have been called to a lifestyle of ministry and evangelism. That means our purpose is at least twofold: ministry and evangelism. Our ministry is to serve others while helping them grow spiritually. Our evangelism is to provide opportunities for nonbelievers to come to know Christ and profess their faith in Him.

This sounds too simple, so let's look at what God says to us in His Word. First, in Paul's second letter to the church at Corinth, we learn, *"Now everything is from God, who reconciled us to Himself through Christ and gave us the ministry of reconciliation: that is, in Christ, God was reconciling the world to Himself, not counting their trespasses against them, and He has committed the message of reconciliation to us"* (2 Cor. 5:18-19).

We minister to others in order to reconcile them to God as God reconciled us to Him. That is the first part of our purpose. We serve each other in ministry for the training of the saints, to build up the body of Christ. Our mission field is wherever God sends us—to work, school, our neighborhood, our community, our state, our country, or lands afar.

You see, God didn't save us to be spectators or nonparticipants in church. He saved us to be ambassadors for Christ, special representatives of His grace to the rest of mankind. With this honorable commission comes the responsibility to always be ready to go wherever He sends us to fulfill His great purpose for our life. If we do nothing, what will the secular world believe about us Christians? Didn't Paul also say that we are our own letter that is openly recognized and read by everyone? We must show integrity in Christ!

Second, we are called to be evangelists—those who are excited and willing to share the gospel of Jesus Christ with others, typically nonbelievers. When Jesus said, *"Feed my sheep," "Follow me I'll make you fishers of men,"* and *"I am sending you,"* He was speaking to all of us. His commands are more specific in Acts 1:8 and Matthew 28:18-20. I encourage you to take a moment right now and review these scriptural passages that confirm these mighty commands. Our purpose is clear: to develop and maintain a lifestyle that includes ministry and evangelism.

We will not be alone in these endeavors. Jesus promised, *"I am with you always to the end of the age"* (Matt. 28:20b). He has empowered us and promised to be with us *always.* We cannot fail! All we really need to do is say, "Yes, Lord. I will be your witness and fulfill the purpose that you have given to me."

In Stage Three of our Spiritual Life Journey, we begin to find a more specific purpose within the realm of ministry and evangelism for which God has called us as individuals. When we learn what our spiritual gift is and begin looking for ways to use it in a mission field, then God will reveal His specific purpose to us according to the grace gift He has given to each of us.

Preparation for old age should begin not later than one's teens. A life which is empty of purpose until 65 will not suddenly become filled on retirement.

Dwight L. Moody, evangelist

Churchgoers are like coals in a fire. When they cling together, they keep the flame aglow; when they separate, they die out.

Billy Graham, evangelist

Chapter 8

SACRIFICIAL LIVING

Offer yourselves to God, and all the parts of yourselves to God as weapons for righteousness.

Romans 6:13b

"*Therefore, brothers, by the mercies of God, I urge you to present your bodies as a living sacrifice, holy and pleasing to God; this is your spiritual worship*" (Rom. 12:1). These words from the Apostle Paul reveal the condition necessary to release our passion and find our purpose for serving our mighty God.

As people establish their passion and purpose and begin to truly live the lifestyle of ministry and evangelism, so many have told me that the sacrifice was just too much, or that they didn't understand what kind of sacrifice was necessary. I agree that this may be one of the most difficult passages of Scripture to understand and follow. Let me explain.

When I was a lost sinner, I lived a life separated from God. He had his priorities for my life and I had mine. My priorities consumed my energies and my focus. When God reached down to me, pulled me towards Him, and caused me to become a believer, I noticed the difference. My heart was changed; now I had to change my lifestyle too. I admit that I didn't move directly to where God wanted me to be and probably not as quickly as I should have. But, little by little, changes began to occur.

First, I had to recognize how different my priorities were from those of God. Second, I had to determine what direction my life should take. Finally, I had to find a way to make my priorities the same as His. If we are to understand what it means to make a "living sacrifice," we must go through this process. For some, it's an easy process; for others, change can be difficult. I believe the strength of our faith will determine how difficult we will find aligning our priorities with those of our God.

There is a great chasm between where we live even as a believing sinner and where God lives in His heavenly realm. How are we to bridge that chasm? First we must recognize the chasm exists. Then we can begin to change our priorities as God changes our heart. This was a slow process for me, as I didn't experience a Damascus Road conversion.

As God began to slowly change my heart, I began to slowly change my priorities. Those things that I so enjoyed doing were beginning to take a back seat to doing those things that I knew pleased God. I had a lot of distractions in my life that consumed my time away from church and ministry. Even though I professed to be a Christian, I still enjoyed a risqué joke, having a cold beer with my friends, and gossiping or complaining about other Christians. These activities began to go away as my focus was coming off self and centering on a loving God who wanted the best for me. He still does!

As my life activities began to reflect God's priorities, I began to feel the joy that comes from being close to Him. The chasm was shrinking. I knew if I stumbled along the way, He would pick me up and set me back on the path that He wanted for me. This move towards God has been and always will be a lifelong process. I don't believe that I will ever be completely across that great chasm until I enter heaven.

One thing is certain. I will continue to make mistakes, but I know that my advocate, who is Jesus Christ, will speak for me and be forgiving of my mistakes. As I look back, I remember the many times that I wasn't a serious Christian. I was involved at church and even taught Sunday School, but Monday through Saturday, I thought little of the One who saved me. I didn't have a faithful or recurring prayer life. My Bible study was almost nonexistent. Sometimes my critical actions towards others were not reflective of an ambassador for Christ. Then God began to change me. I recognized the difference in secular priorities and Kingdom priorities. I determined that my life direction needed to be focused on my ultimate destination in the Kingdom of God. I made my priorities focus on His plan for me and not my own plans. God didn't move. I did!

Today, my prayer life is greatly improved, my Bible study is constant, and I am a much better example of a Kingdom-focused Christian. Once I understood that His plan was for my welfare and the reward was eternal life, I wanted to do what God wanted me to do. I have learned to trust Him more with my life. I learned to step out into the darkness with only His light guiding me—completely trusting Him. I may not be exactly where God wants me to be yet, but I am very close.

When I look back at my lost life, I can see that what I thought were good priorities for me were worthless in the context of eternal life in the Kingdom of God. Once the lifestyle change was made, I didn't even miss those activities that previously occupied my time and focus. The lifestyle I have now has much more joy. I believe that's the result of making this "living sacrifice" for Him. Now that I've done that, I no longer consider any activity that I gave up a material sacrifice. It is just a necessary lifestyle change that reflects my faith in God and my desire to please Him in all that I do. What joy!

You may want to ask yourself the question that I asked long ago. What can I attempt for Him to show my love to Him for what He has done for me through His Son?

Dr. Luke, the Apostle, recorded these words of Jesus Christ: *"If anyone wants to come with Me, he must deny himself, take up his cross daily, and follow me"* (Luke 9:23). In this sentence, I see four action words for us to study. First, there must be a *desire* to follow Jesus. Second, we must be eager to *deny* our own self and the priorities that consume our lives. This will help draw out our passion for service. Third, we must *diligently* take up our cross daily. That is, address and focus on our purpose as frequently as daily. Finally, we must be *devoted* enough to Christ to follow Him wherever He leads.

We cannot take our relationship with Jesus lightly. We must be serious about Him—serious enough to commune with Him on a daily basis. Our willingness to deny self means that we should be prepared to relinquish our own plans, dreams, preferences, and goals, and fully commit to Jesus and His will for our life. That will lead us to total acceptance of the purpose for which we have been saved. To do all of this, we must willingly and deliberately make Christ the first priority in our life.

I encourage you to look for ways to make your lifestyle conform to God's plan for you. When you first accepted Christ and became a Christian, God gave you a passion for service. Once you find the purpose where that passion can be used, your chasm will shrink too. Your priorities will become the same as the priorities that He has planned for you. Your "living sacrifice" will be a joyful journey when you put aside those activities that keep you from Him.

Draw close to Him and let your faith determine your direction. It's a move that will bring you great joy and many rewards.

Questions for Self-Examination

1. *Have you analyzed your priorities to determine if they are Kingdom focused?*

2. *What priorities do you need to change to cross the chasm of separation between you and God?*

3. *Are your priorities moving you towards God? Or are they holding you back?*

4. *Are you living for your purpose or God's purpose for you?*

5. *Have you asked Him to help you identify the priorities in your life that need changing?*

6. *Do you feel spiritual joy for living and serving your purpose?*

If you have faith in the God who called you, you will obey Him, and He will bring to pass what He has purposed to do.

Henry Blackaby, author, speaker, pastor

All of God's people are ordinary people who have been made extraordinary by the purpose He has given them.

Oswald Chambers, theologian

Part Two

EXPRESSING PASSION AND PURPOSE

If we're still uncertain how to develop our own passion and purpose, it may help to see how God helped our spiritual ancestors discover their passion and purpose, as recorded in the Bible. These examples portray how God chose the right people and equipped them for the purpose that He assigned to each of them. You may not have the high calling of these biblical characters, but the calling, the passion, and the purpose are from God. We may be surprised to see that our passion and purpose are often defined in our darkest moments.

Chapter 9

NEHEMIAH'S PURPOSEFUL PASSION

So I prayed to the God of heaven and answered the king, "If it pleases the king, and if your servant has found favor with you, send me to Judah and to the city where my ancestors are buried, so that I may rebuild it."

Nehemiah 2:4b-5

Some 600 years before the birth of our Lord Jesus Christ, God set down a plan of discipline for His unfaithful children. He allowed the Babylonians to come into the Jewish capital of Jerusalem to torment and harass the two remaining tribes of the Jewish faith.

You may remember that the other ten tribes formed the Northern Kingdom after the twelve tribes broke up in the early 900s B.C. Later, God judged this Northern Kingdom using the Assyrians as His tool of punishment. Two hundred years later, the Northern Kingdom no longer existed. The remnant of God's people was in the Southern Kingdom of Judah, but they too became unfaithful to their God.

Just a little over one hundred years after the Northern Kingdom was defeated and forever dispersed by the Assyrians, the Babylonians invaded Judah, destroyed the city of Jerusalem, took the Jewish people captive, and sent them off to Babylonia (now Iraq). It was here that God chose to preserve His remnant of people even though they were enslaved at the time. God is so good. He loves us and saves us even during our time of discipline and punishment.

Seventy years later, God moved again. This time He caused Persia and the Medes to overthrow Babylon. The Jewish people were still enslaved to the new rulers, but God was allowing some new freedoms for His people. According to His plan, the new rulers allowed the Jewish people to return to their homeland. Thus began a one-hundred-year exodus of God's people from the land of Babylonia. They were returning to their homeland! Under King Cyrus of Persia, the temple was to be rebuilt in Jerusalem (2 Chron. 36:22-23; Ezra 1:7). A few decades later, Ezra was sent by the Persian King Artaxerxes to be the spiritual leader of the Jewish people.

By the mid-400s B.C., most of the Jewish remnant had migrated back to their homeland in Judah. The temple was finished and the people were returning to a spiritual relationship with their God. But God was about to move again. He had a plan to help restore the passion and purpose of one of His faithful servants to go back to Judah and rebuild the protective wall around their beloved city of Jerusalem.

Nehemiah was a cupbearer to the King, a man of high esteem in the king's palace located in the Persian city of Susa. He also was a faithful Jewish man of God—a man who had found favor with both his God and King Artaxerxes. He had a passion for serving His God but had not yet found the true purpose that God had designed for him.

Upon hearing from Jewish travelers that the gates to the city of Jerusalem had been burned down and the walls of that great city were laying in rubble, his passion was stirred. Even though Nehemiah had never seen that city in its day of splendor, he had heard the stories from the elders and longed to see the spiritual capital of his people. But when he heard this news, he was so overwhelmed with compassion that he tells us, *"I sat down and wept. I mourned for a number of days, fasting and praying before the God of heaven"* (Neh. 1:4). Now that's passion! In this instance, Nehemiah's passion was in the form of intense mourning for the city of Jerusalem. The intensity of these emotions may have been divinely placed, as he soon sought to redirect his emotions to the greater purpose of helping that city and his people.

Notice that Nehemiah's first response to the rise of passion placed in his heart by God was to fast and pray. He not only prayed for himself, but for all the Jewish people. He confessed his sins and the sins of his people against their Creator. Personal renewal begins with genuine humility and repentance. Then God will hear our prayers and heal us from within. Centuries later, the Apostle Paul too would encourage us to *"pray without ceasing"* (1 Thess. 5:17).

Our passion is not just a suppressed emotion; it's a heartfelt feeling of joy and overwhelming desire to please God. It's initiated by God and brought to surface within us by God. Only our willingness to disobey our God can suppress this passion. If you aren't feeling the same kind of passion for service that Nehemiah felt, I encourage you to improve your relationship with God so that the passion that *you* may have suppressed can come to the surface.

But for Nehemiah, he could only satisfy that burning passion to please God by finding a purpose for the passion he was feeling. Nehemiah reminded God of His promise to Moses: *"If you are unfaithful, I will scatter you among the peoples. But if you return to Me and carefully observe My commands, even though your exiles were banished to the ends of the earth, I will gather them from there and bring them to the place where I chose to have My name dwell"* (Neh. 1:8-9).

God was about to send Nehemiah back to the city of Jerusalem to rebuild the protective wall for the security of His people and His holy temple. He found his purpose! God helped bring out the passion for service in Nehemiah and gave him a great purpose, not only to serve his God, but his people too! His completion of the wall in record time in spite of overwhelming opposition could have only occurred as a result of his divinely inspired passion and purpose.

We are all called to ministry and we are all called to evangelism. We can do neither without a deep passion and clear purpose for serving the God who loves us so much that He is willing to share eternity with us if we'll just be obedient by our repentance, our relationship with Jesus Christ and our works, which may be a reflection of our faith.

Thomas Jefferson once said, "No duty the executive has to perform is so trying as to put the right man in the right place." God doesn't make mistakes! He will always put you in the right place at the right time to accomplish His purpose. All you have to do is recognize the gift He has given to you, release your passion for service, and focus on the purpose for which you have been called.

Recall once again the last words of Jesus spoken just before His ascension: *"You will receive power when the*

Holy Spirit has come upon you . . . " (Acts 1:8a). Good grief! With the power of God upon us, how can we fail? What's our excuse for not recognizing our passion and finding the purpose that God has chosen for us?

If you are unsure of your calling, can't find your passion, or can't discover your purpose, you may need to follow Nehemiah's example. Set aside a time of prayer and fasting. Ask God to show you the spiritual gift He has given to you. Let Him reveal that gift to you and stir your heart with passion. Next, ask Him to reveal the purpose of His calling to you. If you still struggle with this, speak with your pastor who is trained and eager to help you become a serious disciple of Jesus Christ. Fasting will help. Above all, be patient, but don't give up. This process could take more than one prayer session. Your faith is being tested, but you can succeed if your heart is right with God.

All of God's people are ordinary people who have been made extraordinary by the purpose he has given them.

Oswald Chambers, Scottish minister and teacher

God's purpose is greater than our problems, our pain, and even our sin.

Rick Warren, author, speaker, pastor

Chapter 10

PETER'S
UNBRIDLED PASSION

Simon, Simon, look out! Satan has asked to sift you like wheat. But I have prayed for you that your faith may not fail. And you, when you have turned back, strengthen your brothers.

Luke 22:31-32

The Christian church began to spread soon after the ascension of Jesus Christ. In fact, His last command to us was *"You will be My witnesses in Jerusalem, in all Judea and Samaria, and to the ends of the earth"* (Acts 1:8b).

Armed with the power of the Holy Spirit, the apostles heeded this command and began our church. A spiritual awakening was coming and God was setting the stage! In Jerusalem, Peter chose to give his first sermon. We know now that Peter was not the most gifted orator of the chosen twelve. He was more impetuous and a little rough around the edges. Nevertheless, God had chosen him for a mighty purpose.

When Peter stood up in the synagogue to speak, the people must have felt the power of God in him as he began to speak with passion and purpose. *"Let all the house of Israel know with certainty that God has made this Jesus, whom you crucified, both Lord and Messiah"* (Acts 2:36).

The people were astonished! With fear in their voices, they asked, "What shall we do?" Peter's reply is our eternal answer: *"Repent, and let every one of you be baptized in the name of Jesus Christ .... and you shall receive the gift of the Holy Spirit. For the promise is to you and to your children, and to all who are afar off, as many as the Lord our God will call"* (Acts 2:38-39, NKJV).

Yes, the sermon was powerful, but it was more than an oral masterpiece. It reflected Peter's unbridled passion. When you answer God's call, see His purpose in using you, and let your passion shine, you become a magnet for those to whom you direct your passion. That's what happened in Peter's case. Doesn't Scripture tell us that about 3,000 souls were saved that day? Intense passion properly expressed for God's purpose always has amazing results.

But what if Peter didn't see God's purpose for him? What if he tried to speak to the crowd without the passion that was within him? I believe his success would have been significantly less. Passion always creates a passionate response. If God's purpose for you is to lead and you lead with passion, the people will follow. If His purpose for you is to teach and you teach with passion, the response will be passionate too, and spiritual growth in the church will accelerate.

You may be gifted as a server, an encourager, or a giver. Whatever God chooses for you to do, if you do it with passion and purpose, your work will magnify His name and the rewards will be great—for you and the recipients of your work.

Certainly Peter's passion and purpose for serving a risen Christ gave our church a great beginning. But all the apostles shared this passion and purpose as they too were instrumental in accelerating the growth of the early church. *"And the Lord added to the church daily those who were being saved"* (Acts 2:47b, NKJV).

This was quite a turnaround for Peter. Remember it was he who ran and hid from the crowd at the trial of Jesus—shortly after recommitting his life to Him during the Passover meal. Now this apostle, who earlier wanted to kill one of the arresting officers, had seen Jesus after His resurrection and his passion for serving this Master of the Universe was rising fast.

With renewed passion, Peter now spoke with power and authority. He no longer feared the consequences. He had the power of the Holy Spirit and he was going to use it to spread the gospel of Jesus Christ to others. In those days, there was great hostility, even the threat of death to anyone who preached Jesus as the Son of God whose resurrection was for all who believed. Today, that level of persecution still exists in some countries, and we should all be prayerful about entrusting ourselves to others, as Jesus was careful about revealing Himself to those He knew would cause Him harm (John 2:23-25). At the same time, we should recognize our own inadequacies and fears that may be keeping us from acknowledging God's purpose for us.

With the power of the Holy Spirit guiding us, we should be willing to speak boldly on behalf of our Jesus Christ. The worst persecution that many of us will ever face will be the little bit of embarrassment we may feel when our message is rejected. Not everyone who hears our message will accept Jesus and be saved, but we must never give up. We can lead them to the door and let Christ open the door to His Kingdom. It remains their choice to enter or not.

I believe that Scripture guides us to the conclusion that if God puts someone in front of us who needs to hear about Jesus, He has already prepared their heart. The hard part is already over! All we need to do is acknowledge God's purpose and let our passion speak for us.

Many people have told me that they don't have a testimony to share. But I know better. If we believe in Jesus, we can simply tell others what He has done, and is doing, in our lives. Great experience is not required. We can follow Peter's example and let our passion speak for us. Believe me. It can be very contagious.

Prayers prayed in the Spirit never die until they accomplish God's intended purpose.

Wesley L. Duewel, missionary, author, lecturer

Our faith in God ought not to hinder our using whatever means He has given us for the accomplishment of His own purposes.

James Hudson Taylor, English missionary to China

Chapter 11

JOSIAH'S RESPONSIVE PASSION

He did what was right in the Lord's sight and walked in all the ways of his ancestor David.

2 Kings 22:2

Josiah felt his passion for serving his God at the very early age of eight (2 Chron. 34:1). He was not raised in a "church" environment, for his father, King Amon, was a sinful man who worshiped false idols. But Josiah *"did what was right in the sight of the Lord, and walked in the ways of his father David; he did not turn aside to the right hand or to the left"* (2 Chron. 34:2). I find it remarkable that young Josiah felt this passion for the Lord while growing up in an idolatrous household. But God looks at the heart of man and always picks whom He has chosen.

But it wasn't just King Amon who was sinful. All of Judah had become wicked in God's eyes. We have learned that the wickedness of King Amon led to his assassination when Josiah was only eight years old. The people made

Josiah king, and by the time he was sixteen, he had begun to seek the God of David. The closer he drew to his God, the more passionate he would become. It didn't take long for him to reverse Judah's wicked lifestyle. Scripture tells us that at the age of twenty, Josiah *"began to purge Judah and Jerusalem of the high places, the wooden images, the carved images, and the molded images. . . he broke down the altars of Baal and the incense altars. . . He also burned the bones of the priests on their altars, and cleansed Judah and Jerusalem"* (2 Chron. 34:3-5).

Josiah fueled his passion with zealous obedience to God. Because of Israel's idolatry and acts of disobedience, he purged most of the territory of the kingdom of Israel. Once this task was completed, he began to fulfill his purpose for serving God with such great passion. He concentrated on restoring the worship of the God of Abraham to all the people.

Later, when Josiah had reached the age of twenty-six, the high priest Hilkiah found the lost Book of the Law during the repair and cleaning of the temple. It is not the intent of this author to join the debate on the labels of this book. It is sufficient to yield to Scripture's description of this book as the *"Book of the Law of the Lord given by Moses"* (2 Chron. 34:14).

When King Josiah's scribe, Shapham, read the book to the king, Josiah tore his clothes in anguish. Why? Because he loved his God! This book confirmed to King Josiah that his people had not been obedient to the word of the Lord, and it stirred his passion once again to the purpose of restoring Israel to its only true living God. With great passion, he made sure his own household obeyed the Lord's instructions that were found in this recently discovered "bible."

The Chronicles record that Josiah then initiated a nationwide program to eliminate all pagan worship throughout the land, while leading the people to renew their ancient covenant with God. He toured the land, destroyed all likenesses of idolatrous shrines, and celebrated the Passover for the first time in decades. As long as Josiah lived, the people did not depart from following the God of their fathers.

Throughout the thirty-one years of his reign, the people of Israel lived peacefully and worshipped their God. All of this would not have happened if Josiah had not responded to the passion and purpose that God placed on his heart.

We all have this kind of passion given to us at the time we accept Jesus Christ into our lives. Unfortunately, most of us are so successful at suppressing this passion that we cannot see the purpose that God intended it for. Without responding to the passion and purpose for which God saved us, we may as well be the pagan worshipers Josiah encountered in his own country so long ago. Isn't it true that if we don't respond to the gifts that God gives to us and follow His purpose for our life, that we are living a life of disobedience?

Author Richard Owen Roberts[1] identifies at least twelve revival movements in the Old Testament. Each followed a period of disobedience to the Lord. Our disobedience to the Lord results when we turn back from the passion for serving that he has given to us and ignore the purpose of our life in Christ. Are you ready for His judgment today? Wouldn't you rather find your own passion and purpose for serving Him? Jesus begs us to come to Him and *"Share your master's joy!"* (Matt. 25:21). This is not the joy of knowing Jesus; it's the joy of serving Him. There is a remarkable difference in these

1   Richard Owen Roberts, *The Solemn Assembly* (International Awakening Press, 1989).

two joys. There is certainly joy in knowing Jesus, but the latter joy is beyond explanation and is felt only when we are doing precisely what He has called us to do.

Josiah's reward for his faithfulness was the joy of Christ for as long as he lived. God said, *"Because your heart was tender and you humbled yourself before me . . . I will gather you to your fathers, and you will be gathered to your grave in peace"* (2 Chron. 34:27-28). God would spare him from the impending judgment on His people. What a great reward for obedience!

Never forget that life is not about you! You exist for God's purposes, not vice versa.

Rick Warren, author, speaker, pastor

A passion for God isn't necessarily the same as abiding in God; it must be coupled with obedience to be true love for God.

Edwin L. Cole, founder, Christian Men's Network

Chapter 12

JAMES'
THUNDEROUS PASSION

When the disciples James and John saw this, they said, "Lord, do You want us to call down fire from heaven to consume them?"

Luke 9:54

One apostle who exhibited great passion was James, brother of John. Matthew records that James and John were the second set of brothers Jesus called to become apostles.

Jesus gave James and John the nickname "Sons of Thunder," because their passion was often misdirected and seen as anger or hostility. But Jesus saw the potential of these two and called them into His service.

Later, we learn that James' zeal and intensity was put under the guidance of the Holy Spirit, and he became a fruitful member of the inner twelve and a leader in the establishment of the early Christian church.

Finding PASSION *and* PURPOSE

Often we find people who profess to be good Christians and faithful to the church, but their passion is thunderous, intense, and challenging to those around them. If only they would allow the Holy Spirit to re-channel that overzealous passion into positive energy for the Kingdom of God.

We want our passion to be righteous passion. Paul tells us that zeal (passion) without knowledge can be destructive, knowledge without wisdom is dangerous, uncontrolled passion is unproductive, and passion without sensitivity can be cruel.

"I can testify about them that they have zeal [passion] for God, but not according to knowledge. Because they disregarded the righteousness from God and attempted to establish their own righteousness, they have not submitted to God's righteousness. For Christ is the end of the law for righteousness to everyone who believes (Rom. 10:2-4).

Many of us, like James, sometimes let our misguided passion get the better of us. Consider when Jesus was passing through Samaria, as recorded in Luke 9:51-56. As they entered a village to rest for the night, the Samaritans did not welcome Him and offered no place for them to stay.

Now Jesus and His group were headed to Jerusalem to observe the Passover, and the Samaritans believed that all such ceremonies should be observed on Samaria's Mt. Gerizim; thus they refused all accommodations to these travelers.

The passion of the Sons of Thunder turned to outrage at the gall of the Samaritans to refuse accommodations to the One they knew as the Son of God. *"When the disciples James and John saw this, they said, 'Lord, do you want us to call down fire from heaven to consume them?'"* This hostility was unacceptable to our Lord. *"But He turned and rebuked them, and they went to another village"* (Luke 9:54-55). Jesus had come to save, not destroy.

James' passion allowed him to become a close member of Jesus' inner circle of disciples. Scripture tells us that James accompanied Jesus when He raised Jairus' daughter from the dead. He witnessed the transfiguration recorded in Matthew 17:1. He meditated with Jesus on the Mount of Olives (Mark 13:3). He was asked by Jesus to pray with Him privately at Gethsemane (Mark 14:32-33).

All of these events caused James to know Jesus intimately as the true Son of God, and he channeled his robust intensity and passion into serving his Master. This is what Jesus wants from all of us, not just those of us who are as intense and zealous as James was. He wants all of us to find our passion and channel it to His service with sensitivity and compassion for others.

Once our passion comes under the control of the Holy Spirit, we can be effective in our chosen purpose of developing and maintaining a lifestyle of ministry and evangelism. James was still the courageous, zealous person that Jesus called to ministry, but now he was committed to truth and ministry. Christ wants us all to use the qualities that He has given us to serve Him, not for our own selfish enhancement.

James was so passionate in his work to spread the gospel of Jesus Christ, post-ascension, that he aroused the wrath of Herod Agrippa I. James' work helped advance the gospel and the church grew. He had successfully found his passion and purpose for serving a risen Christ. Herod would have none of it. He executed James with the sword as recorded in Acts 12:1-3.

John McArthur said this about James:

James is the prototype of the passionate, zealous, front runner who is dynamic, strong, and ambitious. Ultimately, his passions were tempered by sensitivity and grace. Somewhere along the line he had learned to control his anger, bridle his tongue, redirect his zeal, eliminate his thirst for revenge, and completely lose his selfish ambition. And the Lord used him to do a wonderful work in the early church.

Such lessons are sometimes hard for a man of James' passions to learn. But if I have to choose between a man of burning, flaming, passionate enthusiasm with a potential for failure on the one hand, and a cold compromiser on the other hand, I'll take the man with passion every time. Such zeal must always be harnessed and tempered with love. But if it is surrendered to the control of the Holy Spirit and blended with patience and longsuffering, such zeal is a marvelous instrument in the hands of God. The life of James offers clear proof of that.[2]

What about you? Like James, do you have the courage to ignite your passion for service according to God's purpose for you?

---

2   John McArthur, *Twelve Ordinary Men* (Nashville, TN: W Publishing Group, 2002).

God loves with a great love the man whose heart is bursting with a passion for the impossible.

William Booth, preacher, evangelist,
founder of the Salvation Army

Taking up my "cross" means a life voluntarily surrendered to God.

A.W. Pink, Christian evangelist and scholar

Chapter 13

DAVID'S OBEDIENT PASSION

Then the Lord said [to Samuel], "Anoint him, for he is the one." So Samuel took the horn of oil, anointed him in the presence of his brothers, and the Spirit of the Lord took control of David from that day forward.

1 Samuel 16:12b-13

David is one of the best-known people of all the Scriptures. Unfortunately, he may be best known for his slaying of Goliath, the Philistine giant, and the adultery he committed with Bathsheba. If that is all we remember about this mighty king, then we have missed out on one of Scripture's most passionate men of God.

His passion for obedience to his God allowed him to serve his people Israel and his God for forty years. David's passion for God is proclaimed in Psalm 63:1-3: *"God, You are my God; I **eagerly** seek you. I **thirst** for you; my body **faints** for you in a land that is dry, desolate, and without water. So I **gaze** on You in the sanctuary to see Your strength and Your* *glory. My lips will **glorify** you because your beautiful love is better than life.*" What a passionate declaration from a humble servant!

David was the youngest of eight sons born to Jesse of Bethlehem. Although Scripture doesn't give us a lot of detail about this family, we learn that God chose David to succeed Saul as king of Israel when he was just twelve years old. Why? Samuel, speaking to Saul, told him, *"The Lord has sought for Himself a man after His own heart, and the Lord has commanded him to be commander over His people"* (1 Sam. 13:14, NKJV). That man was David, a person who had passion for loving and serving His Lord.

It would be eighteen years before David actually became king. What he did in those eighteen years is a lesson for all of us who are on a spiritual journey to draw closer to our God. He honed his fighting skills defending his flocks against predatory animals and thieves. He developed musical skills with the flute and harp. He composed poems and songs of praise and worship to honor and glorify his mighty God. We know them as psalms.

Perhaps the most popular of his psalms is the one he wrote about the Good Shepherd:

> *The Lord is my shepherd;*
> *I shall not want.*
> *He makes me lie down in green pastures;*
> *He leads me beside the still waters.*
> *He restores my soul;*
> *He leads me in the paths of righteousness*
> *For His name's sake.*
> *Yea, though I walk through the valley*
> *Of the shadow of death,*
> *I will fear no evil;*

For You are with me;
Your rod and Your staff
They comfort me.
You prepare a table before me
In the presence of my enemies;
You anoint my head with oil;
My cup runs over.
Surely goodness and mercy shall follow me
All the days of my life;
And I will dwell in the house of the Lord forever.

Psalm 23, NKJV

It seems that David was already moving from Stage One of the Spiritual Life Journey to Stage Two. (The four stages of the Spiritual Life Journey are discussed in chapter 3). Sometime during his youth, David became spiritually awakened to His father in heaven. Once he became a teenager, he began to spend more time in prayer and meditation—acquiring and developing a great passion for his God. Samuel had already revealed his purpose as God's chosen heir to the throne of Israel, but it had not yet materialized. That would come with more maturity as God continued to prepare him for his Kingdom role.

As a teenager, David confronted Goliath, the warrior giant of the Philistines. It was not David's strength or courage that defeated this giant; it was his faith in the almighty God of Israel. He challenged Goliath with this message: *"I come against you in the name of the Lord of Hosts, the God of Israel's armies (because) you have defiled Him"* (1 Sam. 17:45). David's great passion and faith in his living God allowed him to challenge this giant without fear. He had spent many years in prayer and meditation with God, and he knew that God would hand over this Philistine to him.

It was during this same time period that David sang, and later penned, the twenty-third Psalm and two others. In Psalm 8 he sang, *"Lord, our Lord, how magnificent is Your name throughout the earth!"* (v. 9). In Psalm 19 he sang, *"May the words of my mouth and the meditation of my heart be acceptable to You, Lord, my rock and my redeemer"* (v. 14). What wonderful passion emitted from this youthful man—words that still bring us joy today, 3,000 years later.

Later, as a grown man, David committed the sin of adultery with Bathsheba. He followed that sin with the sin of murder by having Uriah placed in harm's way during battle so that he would be killed. When the prophet Nathan brought this sin to David's attention, he immediately repented with these words found in Psalm 51: *"Against You – You alone – I have sinned and done this evil in your sight"* (v. 4). He pleaded with God, *"Wash away my guilt, and cleanse me from my sin"* (v. 2); *"Wash me, and I will be whiter than snow"* (v. 7); *"God, create a clean heart for me and renew a steadfast spirit within me"* (v. 10); *"Lord, open my lips, and my mouth will declare Your praise"* (v. 15). This psalm has been an inspiration for repentance for generations.

I believe it was David's great passion for his God that drove him to repent of this dreadful sin against God. The rest of David's life would be filled with trouble externally and internally to his kingdom. Yet his repentance remains a model for all of us who sin.

On the positive side, David had many great accomplishments in fulfilling his purpose for serving God. He conquered Zion and set up Jerusalem as the capital of Israel that stands to this day. He brought the Ark of the Covenant to the new capital city, where David had built a tabernacle. He strengthened Israel with numerous territorial gains and brought the Northern and Southern Kingdoms together under his leadership. Many more accomplishments are recorded in history.

David's passion and purpose for serving his God were evident throughout his long career as a shepherd, musician, poet, warrior, father, and king. But he was far from perfect. We should not dwell on the errors of his life, but on the passion that he felt towards his God. By heavenly inspiration, they have been recorded for eternity. Throughout his whole life, he remained faithful to his God. His loyalty and reverence for God are unquestionable. The poems and songs recorded in Samuel's writings and the Psalms indeed prove Samuel's declaration that David was *"the sweet psalmist of Israel"* (2 Sam. 23:1, NKJV), full of passion and purpose for a deserving God.

When God speaks, oftentimes His voice will call for an act of courage on our part.

Charles Stanley, pastor and author

Prayer is the turning away from ourselves to God in the confidence that He will provide the help we need.

John Piper, theologian, preacher, author

Chapter 14

ESTHER'S
SAVING PURPOSE

*Who knows, perhaps you have come to the kingdom
for such a time as this.*

Esther 4:14b

Nearly five hundred years before Christ was born, a young lady discovered the godly purpose for her life. Esther was an orphan, adopted by her cousin Mordecai from the tribe of Benjamin, which had been conquered by King Nebuchadnezzar of Babylon. At the time of her calling, her family was living in exile in the city of Susa in Persia.

We don't know why Mordecai didn't take his family back to Jerusalem when King Cyrus allowed their return after he defeated the Babylonians. But I believe it was because God had a plan to use them right where they were. I can only guess that it was also God's plan that Mordecai became a court advisor and was well known as someone who "sat in the king's gate." God's hand is present in circumstances even when it is not visible.

Scripture tells us that Esther was a beautiful young virgin. When King Ahasuerus issued an edict that he was looking for a queen, Esther was among the many women who were taken to the palace to "compete" for the King's favor. She did not reveal her ethnicity upon the advice of her guardian, Mordecai. Presumably the king would not have accepted a Jewish woman as queen.

God had other plans, however. After months of preparation, Esther was sent in to the king. She was so beautiful that she *"won approval in the sight of everyone who saw her"* (Esther 2:15). The King was overwhelmed by her: *"The king loved Esther more than all the other women. She won more favor and approval from him than did any of the other virgins. He placed the crown on her head and made her queen"* (Esther 2:17).

Even though she was so favored as to be made queen, she still was not permitted to enter the king's presence without his beckoning. This posed a risky situation for her when God revealed His great purpose for her life.

Haman, an Agagite and member of the royal court, was a puffed-up man of pride who took advantage of his position of power in the king's court and demanded the people bow to him. Mordecai refused. This suggests to us that Mordecai raised his family to be God-fearing and respectful of the Law of Moses, even though this biblical story makes no reference to God. Haman was so angered that he plotted revenge and duped the king into giving him authority to murder all the Jewish exiles in the king's realm.

God, however, had other plans to save his remnant people of Judah. Mordecai asked Queen Esther to plead on their behalf before King Ahasuerus. If she did as Mordecai asked, she risked death for entering the king's presence before he beckoned her and revealing her Jewish heritage. Esther had to move out of her comfort zone to save her people. While these verses don't mention prayer, she did ask Mordecai to *"go and assemble all the Jews who can be found in Susa and fast for me"* (Esther 4:16). In the Old Testament, fasting and prayer go hand in hand, and Esther needed to have God on her side if she was to leave her comfort zone and confront the King.

Because Mordecai and Esther answered the call and responded to God's great purpose for their lives, the people were saved and evil was punished. God was with Esther because it was His plan to save His people from destruction. Sure, we can give credit to Mordecai and Esther for their self-sacrificing acts of courage, but I believe it was God who orchestrated the events from behind the scenes. Once again, He chose to use ordinary people to accomplish His great purpose. Confidence in God's providence and 24/7 presence in our lives are essential for anyone called to accomplish His work and purpose.

God has a purpose for your life just as He did for Esther. Wherever you are, in any situation, He has a plan for you. Serving Him and answering the call may require you to move out of your comfort zone too. Fear not, there is courage from Isaiah: *"Do not fear, for I am with you; do not be afraid, for I am your God. I will strengthen you; I will help you; I will hold on to you with My righteous right hand"* (Isa. 41:10).

The book of Esther is a marvelous, compassionate story of God's redemptive plan to save His people from annihilation. I encourage you to read again this short story that reveals how God uses simple people to accomplish mighty purposes.

God wants to use you wherever you are for His glory. Where is your passion leading you? Be assured that God has a specific purpose for which He wants you to direct that passion. If you don't know the purpose that God has for your life, or yet feel the passion, just ask Him and be confident that He will respond.

Joy is the holy fire that keeps our purpose warm and our intelligence aglow.

Helen Keller, American author and lecturer

Quite possibly there is no greater conformity to the world among evangelical Christians today than the way in which we, instead of presenting our bodies as holy sacrifices, pamper and indulge them in defiance of our better judgment and our Christian purpose in life.

Jerry Bridges, American author and lecturer

Part Three

LEADERSHIP AND RESTORATION

We need to acknowledge that God wants to use each believer to evangelize the unbelieving world and serve Him with the ministry of reconciliation. Our holy Scripture, along with an active prayer life, are the guides that will lead us to a lifestyle of ministry and evangelism as we mature on our spiritual journey. God needs leaders to show the way through this process of renewal and restoration. Under biblical precedent, Christian men of all denominations are asked to assume their natural leadership roles so we all can find our own passion and purpose with a renewed sense of fulfillment.

103

Chapter 15

RENEWAL AND RESTORATION

Draw near to God and He will draw near to you.
Cleanse your hands, sinners, and purify your hearts.

James 4:3

Even after we move into Stage Four of our Spiritual Life Journey, we cannot forget that personal renewal and restoration must come before evangelism. We simply cannot evangelize lost souls if we ourselves haven't renewed and restored our own soul. We must be made righteous in the sight of God, and then we can bring the good news to others by example. We are encouraged by Paul, in his letter to the Ephesians, *"to take [our] stand . . . . with truth like a belt around [our] waist, righteousness like armor on [our] chest, and [our] feet sandaled with readiness for the gospel of peace"* (Eph. 6:14).

Let's look at David's prayer of restoration found in Psalm 51. *"Surely You desire integrity in the inner self . . . wash me, and I will be whiter than snow. Let me hear joy and gladness.*

. . God, create a clean heart for me and renew a steadfast spirit within me. . . Restore the joy of Your salvation to me, and give me a willing spirit. Then I will teach the rebellious Your ways, and sinners will return to you."

I don't know how we can even begin to live out our own passion and purpose unless we continually get on our knees and ask God to purify our own heart. Once we do that, the rest will be easy. We will hear and feel the joy and gladness that God shares with those of us who have been renewed and restored.

I have met so many good, God-loving Christians on my own journey seeking to help other laity restore their passion and purpose for Christ. Time after time, they had an innate resistance to releasing the passion that had built up within them. Often they stated that they wanted to do more, but for some reason, they couldn't take the next step. Their passion for serving Christ was trapped within their own spirituality— unable to find and live the purpose for which He saved us in the first place. How could this be?

First of all, I believe that part of the resistance we all have comes from the roadblocks that Satan puts in front of us to dislodge us from our journey. Second, the men and women that I spoke with admitted fear. I've certainly had my share of that!

But we can overcome that fear and find a way around Satan's roadblocks if we ask God to cleanse us from within. It works for me and it will work for you! I have witnessed hundreds of men and women recommit themselves to Christ as part of their restoration process. This has led them to reach out in their families, communities, and places of work to find new ways to share a newfound joy in Christ. I can only imagine the heavenly choir rejoicing at this good news.

In Paul's letter to the Philippians, he declared, *"For it is God who is working in you, enabling you both to will and to act for His good purpose"* (Phil. 2:13). This is not something we can do ourselves. When we sincerely ask Him to restore in us a clean heart, he will not only cleanse us, but He will lead us to the purpose for which He created us. What joy! What satisfaction!

Covering a period of over six thousand years, and written by forty writers over a period of sixteen centuries, one book, which we call the Bible, portrays God's only plan for mankind. That plan is to reconcile all of us unto Him. What a glorious plan! Unfortunately, millions of people will reject His plan and spend an eternity in hell—separated completely from God.

Those of us who choose God have received, as part of our Christian inheritance, a passion to serve each other and to share the good news of His salvation with our neighbors, whether they live in our family, next door, or across the ocean. I encourage you to release that passion, find your purpose, and get to work. God is waiting for you. He wants you to share His joy and rejoice with Him when others find their passion and purpose.

As I look around the world in the twenty-first century, I see economic chaos, wars, and threats of wars on many continents. Are we getting closer to the time when Christ returns? Perhaps, but we can't waste another minute. The fields are ready for harvest and we need to get busy. God asks so little of us, yet we resist so much. Will your actions today reflect God's purpose in your life?

Questions for Self-Examination

Take a moment to reflect on your personal relationship with God. Does your heart need renewal?

1. *Have you humbly asked God to restore you from within?*

2. *Have you moved beyond the confession of your sin to actual repentance?*

3. *Have you admitted that sin is against God and only Him?*

4. *Have you affirmed that the Word of God is paramount in your life?*

5. *Are you willing to set aside the distractions around you and focus completely on God's calling in your life?*

Read the complete text of Psalm 51 and the first chapter of Nehemiah. Then follow your heart if renewal is needed.

How glorious that, when we resist God's purpose and all but wreck ourselves, He will make us again.

Clovis G. Chappell, PhD, author and minister

God has a purpose in every life, and when the soul is completely yielded and acquiescent, He will certainly realize it.

F.B. Meyer, pastor and English evangelist

Chapter 16

GOD NEEDS LEADERS

He shepherded them with a pure heart and guided them with his skillful hands.

Psalm 78:72

One of my favorite activities in my own spiritual journey is to speak to laymen as I travel throughout the southeastern United States. I believe we men are failing our God in that we are reluctant to get deeply involved in ministry. Too many of us are content to sit in our favorite pew and "play church." That's not what God wants from us! He wants us to be leaders in our homes, in our churches, and in our neighborhoods and places of business. In the days of our Lord's presence on earth, he selected men to be His disciples. Those men were the leaders then, and we should be the leaders now.

It has been proven many times that a family's church attendance follows Dad's attendance. If Dad doesn't go to church, most likely some or all of the same family members will skip church too. If Dad gets involved in church or ministry, family members will follow his leadership. It's not Mom or the children who drive church attendance, it's Dad.

In this regard, we men have failed to show much spiritual leadership in our families. If we can do anything for our God and our families, it's to show by example that we are serious about our relationship with God and to obey His command to develop and maintain a lifestyle of ministry and evangelism.

Yes, the church has evolved over 2,000 years, but this evolution has not taken away our responsibility to God or our families. Church attendance is down all over the Western world because men have lost interest. Divorce rates have skyrocketed because men have lost interest in leading their families. There is widespread corruption and dishonesty in business because men no longer go to work with an attitude of integrity and loyalty. Government is in shambles because the elected leaders no longer feel a responsibility to the people that elected them.

Too often, instead of the four bases of the Spiritual Life Journey, we apply a different kind of baseball analogy to our spiritual relationship with Christ in the church. In baseball, awards are given to those with the highest batting average. Where are the awards for the RBI leaders or the players who scored the most runs? What help does it give the team to hit frequently and get on base if you don't complete the trek around the bases and eventually score?

My favorite baseball team lost many games this year because too many runners were left on base. It takes a team to win games, yet they seldom functioned as a team. The manager refused to play "small ball" and advance leadoff runners with sacrifice bunts. Players often grounded into double plays or struck out with players on base. Yet owners, players, and fans continued to rave about the progress of their players with the highest batting average. It was of little consequence that these same players were not scoring runs. Individual accolades are great, but what about the team? If we men become deacons, teachers, and leaders in our church for personal glory, what happens to the church? How can we grow God's Kingdom without humility, sacrifice, and team spirit? Men, we need to give our all to the church and to our families by giving all the glory to God.

Yet many of us are still content with just getting on first base. We trust that others will take the initiative and help the team (church) get the scores they need. Our pastors seem comfortable with the hitters without regard for the end result. But God wants more RBI leaders and men who will score runs for His Kingdom. He wants leaders who will produce wins and get the best effort from the team. We must change our attitude about scoring runs for our God. Being on first base (sitting in the pew) does little to help our church grow. If our church is to grow at the rate of the early churches, we need more passion from our men. Then we need to channel that passion into a winning purpose for God.

I don't believe our church needs more home-run kings; we just need to have team players who are willing to step up to the plate and do all they can to score runs. Men, we need to get off our hands, get out of the pews, and lead— in our church, in our home, in our business, and in our neighborhood. Jesus needs us to be passionate about serving Him; our family needs us to be loving leaders in our homes to care for our wives and protect our children; our businesses and neighborhoods need us to show *agape* purpose wherever we may be.

Men, are we too fearful of failure to be energized for ministry and evangelism? Sometimes we need to fail in order to succeed. Consider what Michael Jordan of the Chicago Bulls basketball team, in one of his many speeches, tells us about his failures: *"I've missed more than 9,000 shots in my career. I've lost almost 300 games. Twenty-six times, I've been trusted to take the game-winning shot and missed. I've failed over and over and over again in my life. And that is why I succeed."* The best part about serving our loving God is that He doesn't allow us to fail! He gifts us, equips us, and gives us opportunities to "score" without fear because He is always with us—to the ends of the earth.

I believe we must be willing to step out of our comfort zone and learn to use the passion that God has placed on our hearts. Let that passion lead you to a Kingdom purpose, and God will take care of the rest. God's Kingdom will grow, our families will be rewarded, our neighborhoods and businesses will have more successful leadership, and we will experience much more joy than we have ever before felt. We have the joy of knowing Christ and the joy of serving Christ. The latter is a joy beyond description but easily attainable. All we have to do is respond by using what God has already given to us—a passion and a purpose.

THE JOURNEY
CONTINUES . . .

This book has been written with the inspiration of the Holy Spirit to be an encouragement to Christian laity throughout the world to find your passion and purpose in serving God. The late William Carey, a Baptist missionary, preached, *"Expect great things from God; attempt great things for God."* I believe that God has a great plan for your life and we all should strive to fulfill His plan for us as an expression of our thanks for His gift of salvation. This is the unearned gift of His grace.

As you search for your purpose with newfound passion, remember that your primary ministry will be to serve where He has gifted you. Your secondary ministry may be to serve where your church needs you. However, you evangelize wherever God puts you.

Any journey requires careful preparation along with prayer and meditation. You may encounter roadblocks or surprises along the way, but good planning and an earnest desire to succeed will enable you to complete this Spiritual Life Journey.

When we have completed our life calling by serving our Creator with full passion and purpose in the things He has chosen us to do, we can stand before Him and repeat the words of Jesus Christ, *"I have glorified You on the earth by completing the work You gave Me to do"* (John 17:4). How wonderful it would be to hear Him reply, *"Well done, good and faithful slave! You were faithful over a few things; I will put you in charge of many things. Share your master's joy!"* (Matt. 25:23).

Now that you've read this book, I pray that you will reinvigorate your passion to serve God according to His chosen purpose for you, and that you will experience all the joy that is reserved for true disciples of Jesus Christ. May our Holy God bless you as you continue on your own spiritual journey with Him.

Keith Edward Brownfield

Appendix A

STEPS TO FINDING YOUR PURPOSE

If you feel mired in Stage One or Two of your Spiritual Life Journey, and your passion is leading you in a specific direction but you are unsure of the purpose for your life, follow these easy steps to find your ministry.

1. Pray for personal restoration in accordance with Psalm 51.

2. Acknowledge that you have been called to a lifestyle of ministry and evangelism (2 Cor. 6:18; Acts 1:8; Matt. 28:18-20).

3. Accept that God has planned for you a specific ministry (Jer. 29:11) by:

   a. Honestly assessing your life.

   b. Recommitting your life to God.

   c. Trusting God's guidance for your purpose.

4. Develop habits of daily Bible study and prayer that will lead you to greater spiritual maturity.

5. Analyze the abilities, personality, and experiences of your life thus far to determine where God has strengthened you.

6. Discover your spiritual gift (Rom. 12:6-8; 1 Cor. 12:8-10; Eph. 4:11-13).

7. Follow your heart (passion) to His purpose.

8. Learn to be a disciple of Christ (Luke 9:23).

9. Select study material from the reading list in Appendix C and add any books that are not in your current inventory.

10. See where God is working in the area where He purposed you and join Him there.

As you develop your passion to serve God according to His purpose, remember it is for His glory and not yours. Your ministry and service to others in any mission field should always include advancing the Gospel of Jesus Christ and the Kingdom of God.

Appendix B

SPIRITUAL LIFESTYLE WEEKENDS

This is a recommended list of just some of the events available through the North American Mission Board (NAMB) of the Southern Baptist Convention for the spiritual renewal of its laity. The list is not intended to be all inclusive, as many other similar resources are available through your church, regardless of denomination.

The **Lay Renewal Weekend** is an opportunity to reawaken the church to its purpose and passion. It takes believers, wherever they are in their spiritual journey, and refreshes them with a godly perspective of their role in service to others. This is an inward journey that renews and restores the love of Christ to those who have drifted away from their commitment. This weekend also brings the church body together as a family.

The **Lay Ministry Weekend** equips churches by sharing how God has shaped each believer for ministry. Using the acrostic **SHAPE**, this weekend teaches about **S**piritual gifts, what God is continually saying to our **H**eart, and how our **A**bilities, **P**ersonality, and **E**xperiences have uniquely prepared us for specific ministries. Many laypeople understand for the first time that they are just as called to ministry as their pastor. This weekend is preparation for the outward journey.

The **Acts 1:8 Weekend** is a teaching event that leads the church to involve its members in their Jerusalem (local and associational ministries); their Judea (their state convention ministries); their Samaria (national or NAMB ministries); and the ends of the earth (international ministries). This teaching weekend encourages churches to register as an Acts 1:8 Church, a process sponsored by NAMB and IMB that has eight goals for the church to adopt and work toward.

The **Marketplace Evangelism Weekend** is a teaching event that encourages church members to prayer-walk their marketplace (neighborhood, business, or school), asking God how He may want to work through them during the six days they are outside the church walls. Those who commit to God's calling are commissioned by their pastor and church body and sent back into their marketplace as commissioned missionaries from His church, to witness and minister in their unique giftedness.

The **Prayer Empowerment Weekend** is about God's people returning to Him through fervent prayer toward personal holiness and the Great Commission. Participants will also be encouraged and trained in biblical prayer that focuses on Kingdom priorities. Through prayer, God unleashes His church to be in mission with him in their world. The church as a body and its individual members are empowered for whatever God has next for them.

The **Experiencing God Weekend** is a teaching event that introduces a church to the Seven Realities that are explored in the study by Henry Blackaby, Richard Blackaby, and Claude King, *Experiencing God: Knowing and Doing the Will of God* (LifeWay Press, 2007). These spiritual truths reveal how God works through His people to accomplish His purposes. This bestselling discipleship course has helped millions of believers learn to recognize God's activity around them, adjust their lives to Him, and be ready to join Him where He is working.

The **Experiencing God Together Weekend** event provides a catalyst for a church to study the teachings of Henry T. Blackaby and Melvin D. Blackaby in *Experiencing God Together: God's Plan to Touch Your World* (Broadman and Holman, 2002). In this sequel to *Experiencing God: Knowing and Doing the Will of God*, a resource leader shares God's plan for His church to function as Christ's living body, empowered by the Holy Spirit to accomplish God's will and purpose.

The **Called & Accountable** teaching weekend provides an introduction to the study *Discovering Your Place in God's Eternal Purpose*, which demonstrates that God has a unique plan for each of His followers to be a part of His mission. A primary goal of the weekend is to create a sense of understanding in each believer that they are called of God and set apart by God. Just as He did throughout the Bible, God is still calling His people to accomplish His eternal purposes on earth. It is time that all believers realize this truth and commit to be a part of what God is accomplishing on this planet in these days. This event is based on the teachings of Henry T. Blackaby and Norman C. Blackaby in *Called and Accountable* (New Hope Publishers, 2005).

The **Fresh Encounter Weekend** teaching event provides an overview of Seven Phases in God's Pattern for Revival and Spiritual Awakening, which the authors found in Scripture.

The church is introduced to that pattern as they seek to allow the Holy Spirit to lead the church in whatever changes He wants the body to make. The weekend is filled with teaching, testimonies, small group discussions, and prayer. This weekend event is based on the book *Fresh Encounter* (B&H Publishing Group, 2009) by Henry Blackaby, Richard Blackaby, and Claude King.

Appendix C

SUGGESTED READING

The following selections are offered as additional reading to help you find your passionate calling as you seek God's purpose for your life and a stronger relationship with Jesus Christ.

Blackaby, Henry, and Norman Blackaby. *Called and Accountable.* New Hope Publishers, 2005.

Blackaby, Henry, Richard Blackaby, and Claude King. *Experiencing God.* LifeWay Press, 2007; reprinted 2008.

Blackaby, Henry, Richard Blackaby, and Claude King. *Fresh Encounter.* B&H Publishing Group, 2009.

Blackaby, Henry, and Melvin Blackaby. *Your Church Experiencing God Together.* LifeWay Press, 2003.

Fortune, Don and Katie. *Discover Your God-Given Gifts.* Chosen Books, 1987.

Stanley, Charles. *Ministering Through Spiritual Gifts.* Thomas Nelson, 1999.

Rees, Erik. *S.H.A.P.E.* Zondervan Publishing House, 2006.

Taft, Donald C. *The Christian Journey.* AuthorHouse, 2009.

Warren, Rick. *The Purpose Driven Church.* Zondervan Publishing House, 1995.

Warren, Rick. *The Purpose Driven Life.* Zondervan Publishing House, 2002.

ABOUT THE AUTHOR

Keith Edward Brownfield has a passion for helping laypeople find their way around the bases of their Spiritual Life Journey. His vast experience as a Sunday School teacher, discipleship leader, and volunteer missionary with the Mission Service Corps (NAMB/SBC) in the area of lay renewal has helped him find his own passion for serving God.

He has learned firsthand that many laypeople appear to be stuck on the first base of their spiritual journey without knowing why. Drawing upon his own experience of being stuck in the same place for many years and speaking with hundreds of laity yearning to improve their spiritual life, he is led to offer an exciting plan for finding your passion and purpose to serve a loving God.

His unique layman's perspective for helping others find their passion and purpose will be a challenging and entertaining study for the serious Christian. He has been a Christian for over sixty years and currently worships and serves at Spring Valley Baptist Church in Columbia, South Carolina. Keith is available to speak at your church upon request. Additional copies or speaking arrangements may be made at: facebook.com/findingpassionandpurpose.

BUY A SHARE OF THE FUTURE IN YOUR COMMUNITY

These certificates make great holiday, graduation and birthday gifts that can be personalized with the recipient's name. The cost of one S.H.A.R.E. or one square foot is $54.17. The personalized certificate is suitable for framing and will state the number of shares purchased and the amount of each share, as well as the recipient's name. The home that you participate in "building" will last for many years and will continue to grow in value.

Here is a sample SHARE certificate:

HABITAT FOR HUMANITY

THIS CERTIFIES THAT

YOUR NAME HERE

HAS INVESTED IN A HOME FOR A DESERVING FAMILY

1985-2010
TWENTY-FIVE YEARS OF BUILDING FUTURES
IN OUR COMMUNITY ONE HOME AT A TIME

1200 SQUARE FOOT HOUSE @ $65,000 = $54.17 PER SQUARE FOOT
This certificate represents a tax deductible donation. It has no cash value.

YES, I WOULD LIKE TO HELP!

I support the work that Habitat for Humanity does and I want to be part of the excitement! As a donor, I will receive periodic updates on your construction activities but, more importantly, I know my gift will help a family in our community realize the dream of homeownership. **I would like to SHARE in your efforts against substandard housing in my community!** *(Please print below)*

PLEASE SEND ME _____ SHARES at $54.17 EACH = $ $_____

In Honor Of: _____

Occasion: (Circle One) HOLIDAY BIRTHDAY ANNIVERSARY
    OTHER: _____

Address of Recipient: _____

Gift From: _____ *Donor Address:* _____

Donor Email: _____

I AM ENCLOSING A CHECK FOR $ $_____ PAYABLE TO HABITAT FOR HUMANITY **OR** PLEASE CHARGE MY VISA OR MASTERCARD *(CIRCLE ONE)*

Card Number _____ Expiration Date: _____

Name as it appears on Credit Card _____ Charge Amount $ _____

Signature _____

Billing Address _____

Telephone # Day _____ Eve _____

PLEASE NOTE: Your contribution is tax-deductible to the fullest extent allowed by law.
Habitat for Humanity • P.O. Box 1443 • Newport News, VA 23601 • 757-596-5553
www.HelpHabitatforHumanity.org